Clive Bromilow

PROBLEM PLANTS
of South Africa

To Joy and John
with love

Clive

Sponsored by Bayer (Pty) Ltd

Clive Bromilow

PROBLEM PLANTS
of South Africa

Dedicated to my father whom I am sure would have loved this book
Clive Bromilow

Published by:
Briza Publications cc

CK90/11690/23

P.O. Box 56569
Arcadia 0007

First edition 1995

© Clive Bromilow
English edited by Thana Street
Cover design by Tienie du Plessis
Typesetting by McManus Bros, Cape Town
Reproduction by Unifoto, Cape Town
Printed and bound by National Book Printers, Goodwood, Cape

ISBN 0 620 18563 5

CONTENTS

ACKNOWLEDGMENTS

Over the years that it has taken to assemble the contents of this book there have been many, many people who have wittingly and unwittingly contributed to the final product. I would like to acknowledge, where I can, just some of them.

In general I would like to express my gratitude to all my colleagues, past and present, in the agricultural chemical industry. There is a huge store of information and experience in the industry and for various reasons it usually remains as that –in storage. A very large part of this store is still untapped, but everyone I approached gladly gave me the benefit of his/her knowledge and experience. I have spent many days, if not weeks, driving around the country-side with researchers, technical advisers, sales representatives, agents and farmers who have spent a large part of their lives observing weeds and their effects. They are too numerous to mention individually, but to all of them, I offer my sincerest thanks and appreciation.

There have been times when enthusiasm waned and the project seemed to be just too large and complicated ever to be completed. Some people, often with-out realising it, by their words and attitude, gave enormous encouragement which provided the drive to carry on. Margery Moberly at the University of Natal Press sorted out many teething problems in the early days of this book. Prof Andy Cairns always exuded contagious enthusiasm.

To Mike Wells and Leslie Henderson who read parts of the manuscript and offered valuable criticism and advice – thank you. I am grateful also to Marius Fourie for checking the chapter on herbicides and Maude de Matteis for assist-ing with the liaison with Bayer.

I would like to thank the staff at the University of Natal Herbarium – Jane Browning, for her encouragement, but in particular, Trevor Edwards for will-ingly identifying a large number of specimens, when the specimens arrived by the dozen in the early days. A word of thanks also to the staff at the Herbarium of the University of Stellenbosch, especially Mrs Jo Beyers and Mrs Anna Fellingham for dropping their own work to help identify specimens.

My appreciation also goes to Mrs Thana Street for her professional editing of the text.

I would also like to express my appreciation to Frits van Oudtshoorn for his confidence in me and the book. The assistance and advice he offered along the way, especially with the grasses, which are his speciality, always served as inspiration and encouragement.

Finally, I would like to thank Bayer for their confidence and faith in me and in the project and, not least of all, for the financial support that made the whole project come together as an affordable and worthwhile end product.

Clive Bromilow

FOREWORD

The great beauty of South Africa, with its diverse fauna and flora has been well documented in numerous pictorials and other publications. Understandably, the compilation of adequate guides for the identification of weeds or unwanted plants has not received the same attention, although they represent an integral part of our environment.

The same climatic diversity of southern Africa that provides a suitable environment for our splendid flora and wide range of crops, also creates living conditions for an equally diverse range of weeds.

During his working life as an agriculturalist in South Africa and further afield in numerous countries throughout the world (in East Asia, the Middle East, USA, Europe and Northern Africa) Clive Bromilow, who compiled this guide, has experienced difficulties in identifying weeds and other pests. This gave him an appreciation of the problem and inspired him to embark on this project. Proper identification, of course, is the first step in undertaking adequate control measures, and I am confident that this well–illustrated and comprehensive guide on the problem plants of southern Africa will satisfy this demand.

I trust that this publication will stimulate the interest of agriculturalists and nature lovers alike in the identification of weeds, not only in agricultural crops, but also where they occur in people's gardens and daily lives.

The Crop Protection Division of Bayer is proud to support this effort.

Martin Petersen
Manager: Crop Protection Division
Bayer (Pty) Ltd, South Africa

INTRODUCTION

A weed is a plant in the wrong place at the wrong time. Any plant can be a weed: pretty ones, ugly ones, rare ones, even crop plants such as maize or wheat. A weed must be a nuisance, just sometimes.

Plants that become weeds are usually vigorous growers, making them compete for water, light, space and nutrients. They are adaptable, being able to easily invade a wide range of ecological niches. Most of them are exotic or foreign in origin. They are tough and can withstand unfavourable conditions. They are easily spread, producing an abundance of fertile seeds or other propagules often with efficient methods of dispersal. The most frustrating characteristic is that, for a number of reasons, they are often difficult to control.

Any plant, with one or more of these characteristics, may easily become a nuisance to man, compete with his crops for precious water and nutrients etc. They also clog his machines, interfere with and poison him or his animals, act as hosts for crop diseases and insect pests, upset the natural indigenous ecology or otherwise offend man's aesthetic senses.

The plants in this book are just some of those that occur in South Africa. Many relatively common weeds may not be included and there will be others where inclusion may not seem to be justified. The general criteria used to judge if a species warrants inclusion are the following:

a) Economic importance.
b) Mention on commercial herbicide labels.
c) Exotic origin.

Detailed botanical descriptions are avoided. Only important or interesting characteristics are mentioned in the text, and identification is left to the illustrations. The text includes such information as origin, distribution, pest status, methods of control, or anything of specific interest.

Many plants have distinctive seedlings and often early identification is important so that suitable control measures can be initiated before a weed has become established. Where appropriate, pictures of the seedlings are included. Likewise, where many plants have distinctive vegetative growth or characteristic flowers, their main features are shown in the illustration.

Where available, each weed has been given the common Afrikaans and English names and their names in the various black languages. Many farmers refer to weeds by their names in the black languages or other common names which are not included here. For instance, *Cynodon dactylon* is known to have some 65 English and Afrikaans names as well as 14 recorded names in the black languages – and this just in South Africa.

Everybody is affected by weeds in some way. Not everybody, however, has access to a simple means of identifying the weed that for whatever reason, has caught his/her attention. Whether you are a farmer, gardener, city dweller, agricultural researcher or extension officer, school pupil or university scholar, layman or expert, this book will guide you towards the identity and background of the plant of interest.

The identities of the plants in the photographs were usually determined by or with the assistance of herbaria staff around the country, referring to literature and comparing collected specimens with material in the herbaria collections. Although every effort has been made to ensure that the identifications are accurate, they are, however, not guaranteed. Remember also, that a plant species may appear considerably different in colour or form under different growing conditions. Conversely, there are sometimes closely–related species that appear superficially identical. If the positive identification of a weed is required, refer to a detailed botanical book or take a specimen to an expert.

The background information contained in the text was drawn from published literature, colleagues in the agrochemical industry, farmers, researchers and from personal experience. To the best of my knowledge this information is true and correct. However, this book is a guide, not a scientific or botanical reference – please treat it as such.

ABOUT THIS BOOK

ARRANGEMENT

The species in this book are grouped into families. The name of these families is in capital letters at the beginning of each text with the names usually ending in –aceae.

The grasses (Poaceae family) are listed first, followed by the rest of the monocotyledons. Then, beginning with the Aizoaceae, come all the dicotyledon families in alphabetical order. Following the dicotyledon families are the Pteridophyte families (ferns), with Bracken fern the only inclusion. The final group are all the water weeds, and although not always closely related, they are included as a group because of their specific preference for water. Within each family the species are also arranged alphabetically.

Where more than one species is associated with one section of text, they appear in alphabetical order.

At the end of this chapter is a list of all the families represented in this book. Each family is described using commonly known names or typical, familiar examples.

PHOTOGRAPHS

The photographs show typical examples of common species of weeds. Where suitable, closely–related species are mentioned in the text. Positive identification would, however, only be possible with a much closer examination of an actual specimen.

The photographs are taken from angles and distances to show:

    a) Typical specimens
    b) Characteristic features and situations
    c) Size and scale.

SPECIES TEXT

To assist further with determining scale, each species text includes the plant's 'average' height. This is not the maximum height, but the height a species might usually achieve when it is growing unhindered and in favourable conditions. The height given for a spreading species, is the usual height of the aerial parts above the ground and, for a climbing species, the common height to which a specimen could climb.

Where suitable, distinguishing features are mentioned in the text. Otherwise identification, as far as is possible, is left to the photograph.

NAMES

The botanical or latin names are those that are published in 'Plants of southern Africa: names and distribution,' 1993.

To the non–botanist it may be difficult to understand why plant names are always changing. It is because botanists are continuously studying all plant species and sometimes find it necessary to make adjustments. For example, large families may be sub–divided, smaller families may be combined or a species can be moved to a family to which it is more closely–related than another. Previous or outdated botanical names are in parentheses after the current one. In most cases, name changes older than about 10 years are not mentioned.

The common names are those which in my experience and in most of the publications listed, are the names by which a plant is most commonly known. Where there is doubt as to the most frequently used name or where there is a very frequently used but localised name, more than one name is mentioned. Occasionally a name commonly used in the black languages is mentioned. There will, of course, be many other names not mentioned here.

TEXT STYLE

This book is written for use by all, including and perhaps especially for those who are not familiar with botanical terminology. For this reason botanical terms are avoided if at all possible. Where such use is unavoidable or it adds interest to the text, an explanation is often included with the word together with a further explanation in the glossary.

The glossary also includes non–botanical words that need defining. e.g. 'common', 'cosmopolitan' or 'alien'.

WEEDS AND THEIR CONTROL

WHAT IS A WEED?
A weed is a plant that is growing in an undesirable place.

WHEN IS A PLANT A WEED?
A plant can be a weed if it does one or more of the following things:

1. It interferes directly with crops by:
   a) Competing for available nutrients, moisture or light.
   b) Physically interfering with the growth of the crop.
   c) Interfering with the harvesting process.
   d) Contaminating the final product such as with seeds or by tainting.
2. It interferes indirectly with crops by harbouring insect pests or diseases which attack such crops.
3. It harbours or encourages insects that may pose a threat to health.
4. It is poisonous to man or his domesticated animals.
5. It is a foreign or exotic invader, thereby upsetting the indigenous ecology.
6. It interferes with the recreational use of certain areas such as golf greens and water areas.
7. It is unsightly or obstructs vision as, for example on roadsides.
8. It is a general nuisance, as in gardens.

HOW DOES A PLANT BECOME A WEED?
For a plant to become a weed, it needs to possess one or more of the following characteristics. (These characteristics will tend to be those that set a weedy plant apart from a non–weedy one):

1. Efficient methods of dispersal.
2. The ability to establish itself easily.
3. Rapid and efficient reproduction.
4. Rapid growth.
5. A well–developed and deep root system.

6. Adaptability, i.e. being able to grow in a wide variety of habitats.

7. Aggressiveness as a competitor.

8. Hardiness, i.e. being able to withstand adverse growing conditions.

9. It is difficult to eradicate.

CONTROL OF WEEDS

For literally thousands of years, man has been combating undesirable plants with every means at his disposal. From the early days when only physical means were available, to modern times when man has at his disposal a whole armoury of effective techniques, from machines to the technology of biological control and an enormous array of highly sophisticated chemicals.

There are four basic methods by means of which weeds are controlled:

(i) PHYSICAL

    a) Chopping and slashing.
    b) Digging or bulldozing.
    c) Cultivation or hoeing.

(ii) CULTURAL

This is the adaptation of the weeds' environment by such things as:
    a) Crop rotation.
    b) The use of catch crops.
    c) Winter ploughing.
    d) Irrigation management.
    e) The use of fire.

(iii) BIOLOGICAL

This is the use of naturally occurring biological agents, such as:
    a) Insects that can eat the foliage or seeds.
    b) Diseases.

(iv) CHEMICAL

See "Chemical Weed Control" .

CHEMICAL WEED CONTROL

CHEMICALS AND THE LAW
Today a wide range of sophisticated chemical herbicides are sold under an even wider range of trade names. The use of these products requires specialised knowledge. Before any herbicide is used, an expert should be consulted. The label on the container should always be read carefully and understood. Anyone intending to use a herbicide must bear in mind the proclamation made by the Minister of Agriculture in Government Gazette No 13424 dated 26.07.92 which states that it is an offence to:

"..... acquire, dispose, sell or use an agricultural or stock remedy for a purpose or in a manner other than that specified on the label on a container thereof or on such a container".

Any claim on a herbicide label must be approved by the Registrar, backed up by conclusive data and registered in accordance with the Act known as the Fertilizer, Farm Feeds, Agricultural Remedies and Stock Remedies Act No. 36 of 1947. This Act is intended to cover and protect the user, manufacturer, and supplier of a product, the general public and the environment. The implications of the Act are wide-ranging, but as far as product labels are concerned, the label is in effect a legal document. Any deviation from the prescribed label is therefore a contravention of the Act.

Although there is a wide range of products with a wide variety of weeds on the labels, there is still a large number of common and often extremely troublesome weeds that are not mentioned on any product label. There are also many minor crops or situations for which products have not been specifically registered. As mentioned above, all products must undergo intensive testing and only proven effects are admissible on a label.

Most of the weeds in this book have one or more herbicides registered for their control. If possible, this is mentioned in the text, along with a mention of techniques needed to apply the herbicide. Where no herbicides are actually registered for a weed and it is known that one of the other methods is effective, this is also mentioned. This book must also conform to Act 36 of 1947, therefore no claims can be made about chemicals or chemical control that do not appear on a herbicide label.

CHEMICALS FOR THE CONTROL OF WEEDS
This is an outline of the types of chemical products currently available and some of the common terms used to describe them:

HERBICIDES
A herbicide is a substance, either naturally occurring or man–made, that

alters the metabolic processes of a plant so that the plant is suppressed, killed or its growth altered in such a way that it becomes less of a problem. Herbicides may be divided into groups according to their general mode of action:

Non-selective vs selective herbicides

Non-selective – These herbicides will affect any plant with which they come into contact. For instance, some of these chemicals can act by destroying chlorophyll.

Selective – These chemicals can kill a weed without harming a crop, even if it is sprayed over the top of the crop. (One can use a non-selective chemical in a selective manner such as for inter–row treatment, but this does not alter these basic divisions.)

Contact vs systemic

Contact – These are products that act by affecting only the plant tissue with which they come into direct contact. Thorough coverage and wetting of the weed is necessary for effective control. Many plants become more tolerant of such chemicals as they mature. Seedlings are usually very sensitive, whereas perennial plants which can regrow from the remaining roots, can recover.

Systemic – These chemicals are translocated throughout the plant from the initial site of application. For instance, a chemical applied to the foliage can be translocated to the roots and if sufficient quantities have been applied, the whole plant is destroyed, including tough perennial root systems.

Pre– vs post– emergence

Pre–emergence – A pre-emergence herbicide is applied to the soil before the weeds emerge. Uptake is usually by the growing coleoptile (shoot), or by the developing roots.

Post-emergence – These herbicides are applied after emergence of the weeds and usually have a high degree of leaf uptake. To a certain extent this term is also used to describe products applied to mature plants.

Long vs short residual action

Some products can remain active in the soil for many months or even years, whereas others have a relatively short life. Some chemicals are deactivated almost immediately on contact with the soil.

CHEMICAL GROUPS

There are many different chemical groupings at present and no doubt, new ones will continue to be discovered. The following are some of the more important chemical groups:

Triazines and Ureas

The members of these groups are usually soil-applied, residual herbicides, acting by the inhibition of photosynthesis. They do not affect germination but are taken up by the developing roots, with a plant often only showing symtoms of poisoning after emergence and actually dying of starvation. These chemicals normally have a fairly wide range of activity, but are usually better at controlling broadleaf weeds than grasses.

Acetanelides (Amines).

This group acts by inhibiting protein synthesis, disturbing cell division and affecting the cell membrane. They can therefore prevent germination but will also work by inhibiting root and overall growth. The members of this group are primarily grass killers with a variable effect on broadleaf weeds and sedges (e.g. nutgrass).

Phenoxy compounds

This group is also sometimes referred to as the 'hormone' group, acting primarily as artificial plant hormones and upsetting the hormone balance within the weed. This imbalance causes uncontrolled cell division and enlargement in the growth point of the plant. It consequently induces a large number of biochemical and metabolic changes that lead to abnormal plant development. The phenoxy compounds are principally killers of broadleaf weeds.

Thiocarbamates

The chemicals in this group are volatile and must be incorporated into the soil to prevent loss by evaporation. They show a high degree of selectivity and have a relatively long residual action. They are absorbed by the growing coleoptile so they do not prevent germination but should prevent emergence. They are active mainly on grasses and sedges and are often used to control red and yellow nutgrass.

Dinitroanalines

The dinitroanalines are somewhat less volatile than the thiocarbamates. Some, however, still require incorporation into the soil and have a long residual action. These chemicals are mainly grass killers.

Sulphonyl Ureas

The first products in this group were only developed during the 1980s and started a whole new era in chemical weed control. They are highly active at very low dosage rates, often being effective at rates as low as 10 g per hectare. Although the first sulphonyl ureas were mainly post–emergence broadleaf weed killers, this group now contains products with a wide range of herbicidal actions.

Phosphorous herbicides
Typified by glyphosate and its salts. Discovered in the early 1970s, this group currently enjoys the largest volume of usage of any group of herbicides. They are post–emergence, non-selective and systemic products and act by inhibiting the formation of amino-acids. On contact with the soil these products lose their herbicidal qualities and are broken down by soil micro–organisms into carbon dioxide, nitrogen, water and phosphate.

Bipyridylium compounds
A small, but very widely used group of herbicides typified by the chemical paraquat. They are non-selective, post–emergence and contact herbicides. They are rapidly absorbed by green plant tissue with only partial translocation. On contact with the soil they are immediately deactivated by being adsorbed onto clay particles.

Adjuvants or 'Surfactants' (Surface-active chemicals such as wetters, stickers, spreaders etc.).

This is a group of chemicals that are added to spray mixtures to enhance the effect or properties of the chemicals to which they are added. Sometimes the use of one of these products is specifically recommended, and sometimes it is important that they are not used. (Most herbicides have various types of surfactants already in the formulation, therefore it is important to read the labels carefully.):

Wetters – In general terms, a wetter is a substance that reduces the surface tension of a spray droplet. This, for example, allows the droplet to spread over and adhere to a waxy or hairy leaf surface. This has implications for the water volume applied and for the possibility of run-off. Many of these products are based on soaps and detergents.

Stickers – A sticker is a surfactant which improves the retention of spray droplets once good wetting and coverage has been achieved. Stickers tend to dry and should not dissolve again too quickly in water. They can improve the rain fastness of applied products.

Penetrant – A penetrant increases the penetration of the active ingredient of an applied product into the target. This requires absorption into the cuticle, movement across the cuticular membrane and absorption by the underlying cells.

Stabilisers – A stabiliser promotes and maintains uniform distribution of the active ingredient throughout the spray tank. Most herbicide formulations already contain a range of chemicals such as emulsifiers, dispersants, solubilisers etc. There are, however, products available that can be added to a spray mixture to enhance the effect described above.

Compatibility Aids – There are one or two products that can be added to a spray mixture in order to prevent a chemical reaction or physical changes from occurring. They may influence the efficacy of the other products in the mixture.

Buffers – Buffers maintain the desired pH of spray mixtures in the tank. Some pesticides, particularly some types of insecticides and fungicides, degrade rapidly in alkaline conditions (high pH). Most modern products are relatively stable in a pH of 6 but the optimum pH would appear to be about 4,5. Herbicides are generally less sensitive to a high pH and do not normally require the addition of a buffer. Please note, however, that a buffer is not an acidifier.

Drift Control Agent – Such an agent controls the size of spray droplets by various means, one of which is by the reduction of evaporation. These products are particularly valuable for aerial application where low spray volumes with small droplets are used and droplet size must be maintained in order to reduce wastage and drift.

FACTORS THAT INFLUENCE EFFECTIVE WEED CONTROL

Successful weed control depends on the correct choice of method or product and the proper application thereof. There are many factors that influence the efficacy of chemical herbicides:

FACTORS THAT AFFECT MANY SOIL-APPLIED HERBICIDES

Fineness of the seedbed – A fine seedbed encourages even germination and even distribution of the herbicide.

Soil moisture or rainfall – Soil-applied herbicides usually need a certain level of moisture or even need to be washed into the soil by rain or irrigation before they can start to work.

Clay percentage – Most soil-applied herbicides are chemically adsorbed by clay particles, thereby rendering them inactive. Usually, the higher the clay content, the more herbicide must be applied to compensate for this loss.

Humus or organic matter content of the soil – The organic fraction of soil acts in the same way as clay but is an even stronger adsorber of chemical ions.

Soil pH – Soil pH can affect the rate of breakdown and thereby the residual effect of some chemicals.

Timing in relation to weed germination – Weeds that have already germinated may not be controlled, especially by pre-emergence herbicides.

Depth of germination – A weed germinating very close to the surface may escape the herbicide if the chemical has been washed into the soil. Conversely, a weed germinating at depth may escape if uptake of that particular product is mainly by the roots and the chemical is not washed in.

Application method – The type and accuracy of the equipment used is of the utmost importance.

FACTORS THAT AFFECT FOLIAR-APPLIED HERBICIDES

Development stage of the weed – Seedlings are very sensitive to these chemicals, especially the contact type herbicides. Systemic herbicides require a large leaf area and active plant growth for efficient translocation.

The vitality of the plant – Plants under stress cannot efficiently absorb or translocate a herbicide.

Climate – This affects plant vitality. Rain, for example, can wash a chemical off before it has been taken up.

Product mixtures – Sometimes wetting agents must be added to foliar–applied herbicides, thereby enhancing the adherence of spray droplets to the leaves, especially waxy ones. Sometimes if a mixture of products is used, one of the products may interfere with the action of another. Conversely, some chemicals have a synergistic effect on others with the result that a mixture can be more active that the sum of the individual components.

Application method and degree of wetting – Suitable equipment and sufficient water if necessary, should always be used for required coverage.

REMEMBER: Always read the label first, use the product accordingly and follow all instructions relating to the safe and proper use and storage of the product. It is against the law to do otherwise.

A herbicide can only work well if it is applied correctly, therefore a thorough knowledge of the principles of application is also required. If in doubt, consult an expert or the supplier.

COMMON NAMES OF PLANT FAMILIES

Aizoaceae – the *Tetragonia* family
Alliaceae – the *Agapanthus* family
Amaranthaceae – the cockscombs and amaranth family
Apiaceae – the carrot family
Araceae – the arum lily family
Asclepiadaceae – the asclepia, milkweed and *Stapelia* family
Asparagaceae – the asparagus family
Asteraceae – the daisy and sunflower family
Basellaceae – Madeira vine
Bignoniaceae – the tecoma and jacaranda family
Boraginaceae – the forget-me-not and borage family
Brassicaceae – the mustard family
Cactaceae – the cactus family
Cannabaceae – the hemp family
Capparaceae – the caper and *Cleome* family
Caryophyllaceae – the carnation family
Chenopodiaceae – the beet, spinach and goosefoot family
Clusiaceae – St John's wort
Commelinaceae – the commelina and spiderwort family
Convolvulaceae – the morning glory and bindweed family
Crassulaceae – the *Crassula* and stonecrop family
Cucurbitaceae – the pumpkin family
Cyperaceae – the sedges
Dennstaedtiaceae – the bracken fern family
Euphorbiaceae – the *Euphorbia* or spurge family
Fabaceae – the pea, bean or pod-bearing family
Fumariaceae – the fumitory family
Geraniaceae – the geranium family
Haloragaceae – the parrot's feather (aquatic) family
Illecebraceae – the annual scleranthus family
Iridaceae – the iris family
Lamiaceae – the sage and mint family
Malvaceae – the *Hibiscus* and cotton family
Meliaceae – the syringa family
Mesembryanthemaceae – the vygie family
Myrtaceae – the myrtle and *Eucalyptus* family
Nyctaginaceae – the bougainvillea family
Onagraceae – the fuschia family

Oxalidaceae – wood sorrel and bermuda buttercup family
Papaveraceae – the poppy family
Passifloraceae – the passion-flower and grenadilla family
Pedaliaceae – the sesame family
Phytolaccaceae – the pokeweeds
Pinaceae – the cedar family
Plantaginaceae – the plantains
Poaceae – the grasses
Polygonaceae – the rhubarb and sorrel family
Pontederiaceae – the water hyacinth family
Portulacaceae – the *Portulacca* and purslane family
Primulaceae – the primrose family
Proteaceae – the *Protea* family
Resedaceae – the mignonette family
Rosaceae – the rose family
Rubiaceae – the *Gardenia* family
Rutaceae – the rue family
Salicaceae – the willow family
Salviniaceae – the Kariba weed (aquatic) family
Sapindaceae – the soapberry family
Scrophulariaceae – the snapdragon and foxglove family
Solanaceae – the potato, tomato, tobacco and nightshade family
Sterculiaceae – the *Sterculia* family
Tiliaceae – the jute family
Typhaceae – the bulrush family
Urticaceae – the nettle family
Verbenaceae – the *Verbena* family
Zygophyllaceae – the creosote bush and *Tribulus* family

MONOCOTYLEDONAE

POACEAE

Aristida congesta subsp. *barbicollis*
Spreading three-awn, Lossteekgras

Aristida congesta subsp. *congesta*
Tassel three-awn, Katstertsteekgras

Aristida junciformis
Ngongoni three–awn, Ngongoni–steekgras

Height: 50 cm

Both subspecies of *A. congesta* are indigenous and widespread in South Africa. They occur mainly in overgrazed or tramped-out veld, in gardens, croplands, waste areas and on roadsides.

A. junciformis is a very tough and unpalatable grass which increases and forms dominant stands in overgrazed veld. It prefers high rainfall areas and can be a serious invader, particularly in some parts of Natal and the Eastern Province.

The seeds of *Aristida* spp. penetrate socks and clothing and can severely damage the fleece of sheep and angora goats.

These weeds are susceptible to industrial herbicides used on roadsides.

POACEAE

Arundo donax
Giant reed, Spaanseriet

Height: 6 – 10 m

This perennial plant from Eurasia, is now a weed in the eastern parts of South Africa, especially the Transvaal Lowveld.

The Giant reed was probably introduced for ornamental purposes as it can reach enormous heights. It is not often seen to flower. This reed must not be confused with the indigenous *Phragmites australis* (Common reed/Gewone fluitjiesriet), or *Phragmites mauritianus* (Lowveld reed/Laeveldfluitjiesriet). The latter two species of reeds are much less robust and lack the large leaf lobes of *Arundo*.

Phragmites can grow in water up to a depth of one or two metres, interfering with recreational use, blocking waterways and increasing stagnancy. In such moist areas *Phragmites* outperforms *Arundo* which favours moist, but not wet places. They all have strong underground rhizomes and can take root if the stems are cut and used as stakes.

Aristida congesta subsp. barbicollis

Aristida junciformis

Arundo donax

25

The Giant reed is an untidy plant but, as with the reeds can be highly beneficial in the right place. They can act as erosion control agents, filtering muddy flood waters and be havens for a wide range of wildlife.

All these reeds are very difficult to control. Physical methods must include total removal of the rhizomes as the plants can regrow from pieces left in the soil, even when under 1 – 2 m of water.

It is possible to control these reeds with chemicals. They should be cut down to water or ground level. The lush regrowth must be sprayed with a systemic herbicide when it has reached a height of 1 – 2 m. Good coverage with the recommended herbicide is essential for optimum results. Thorough follow–up treatments are required for effective long–term control.

Observe any restrictions on the herbicide label as regards subsequent water use.

POACEAE

Avena barbata
Slender wild oats, Wildebaardhawer

Avena byzantina
Red oats, Rooihawer

Avena fatua
Common wild oats, Gewone wildehawer

Avena sterilis
Tall wild oats, Groot wildehawer

Height: 1,5 m

These closely related, major grass weeds occurring all over the world, have been introduced into South Africa from Europe or Asia. *A. fatua* and *A. byzantina* are the species most commonly occurring in the summer rainfall region, the latter being less susceptible to herbicides. *A. sterilis* is usually found in the winter rainfall areas.

Wild oats are prevalent in most wheat–growing areas, especially where 'wheat on wheat' methods are followed e.g. in the O.F.S. and Cape Province. In the winter rainfall region, winter ploughing helps to reduce the weeds but this can only be done in the absence of winter wheat. Wild oats are not common in areas such as Natal where wheat tends to be grown under irrigation and in rotation.

Wild oats can be identified at an early stage in a wheat field by their flatter growth habit, relatively long ligules and hairs at the base of the leaf. They have a distinctive seed and must not be confused with volunteer commercial oats (*Avena sativa*).

Wild oats are usually spread by means of contaminated wheat seed and with machines such as combine harvesters.

Avena fatua

The ability of wild oats seed to lie dormant in the soil for about nine years, makes the weeds extremely difficult to control by means of crop rotation. In winter wheat under dryland conditions they are extremely difficult to control chemically and selective post–emergence herbicides must be used. Furthermore, since wild oats are closely related to cereal crops, it means that the registered herbicides (of which there are several), need to be highly selective and specialised.

POACEAE

Bothriochloa insculpta
Pinhole grass, Stippelgras

Height: 75 cm

Pinhole grass is an indigenous grass that is very common in the warmer areas of the summer rainfall region. It is perennial and has a characteristic and very prominent hairy node.

Pinhole grass does not invade annual croplands, but can often be found in orchards and on roadsides, often in high densities. In overgrazed veld it can increase to the extent that it dominates all other grasses as it is not very palatable.

No specific herbicides have been registered for this grass.

POACEAE

Brachiaria deflexa (=Pseudobrachiaria deflexa)
False signal grass, Bastersinjaalgras

Brachiaria eruciformis
Sweet signal grass, Litjiesinjaalgras

Height: 40 cm

These *Brachiaria* species are fairly widespread, common and indigenous annual grasses. *B. eruciformis* tends to restrict itself to damper sites and turf soils and is more common in the Transvaal and O.F.S. than elsewhere. Signal grass is sometimes a weed of lands and gardens but seldom becomes a serious problem.

B. deflexa with its characteristic broad leaves, is found mainly in the Transvaal in moist, shady areas. False signal grass is somewhat less weedy than sweet signal grass.

These grasses are susceptible to many pre–emergence and post–emergence grass killers and are controlled by shallow cultivation during the seedling stage.

Bothriochloa insculpta

Brachiaria deflexa

Brachiaria eruciformis

29

POACEAE

Briza maxima
Large quaking grass, Bewertjies

Briza minor
Small quaking grass, Kleinbewertjies

Height: 50 cm

Quaking grass represents two species of annual grass introduced into South Africa from the Mediterranean region, probably as ornamentals, having attractive flower heads that are used in flower arrangements.

The quaking grasses have become naturalised and are now found throughout the southern Cape Province, where they are common.

Both species are weeds of roadsides, orchards and gardens. They occasionally appear in irrigated crops. Quaking grass rarely becomes very competitive unless left unattended.

The plants are susceptible to many herbicides and will succumb to cultivation, especially during the seedling stage.

POACEAE

Bromus catharticus (=B. willdenowii/B. unioloides)
Rescue grass, Brome grass, Reddingsgras

Height: 1 m

Rescue grass is a common and widespread weed from South America that has invaded pastures, orchards, vineyards, roadsides and waste places.

Rescue grass grows vigorously in winter but requires moisture and low grazing pressure to flourish. Although palatable, it does not compare to ryegrass in performance, with the result that it is undesirable in pastures. It can also be a problem in winter grains such as wheat and plays an important role in the life cycle and survival of the Russian wheat aphid in the O.F.S.

In pastures or grass crops such as wheat, highly selective herbicides are required to control this grass. In other areas rescue grass is susceptible to the usual chemicals. It is also easily removed by cultivation.

Briza maxima

Briza minor

Bromus catharticus

31

POACEAE

Bromus diandrus
Ripgut brome, Predikantsluis, Langnaaldbromus

Bromus pectinatus (=B. japonicus)
Japanese brome, Hooigras

Height: 40 cm

Originally from the Mediterranean region, this species has been introduced into South Africa and has spread rapidly, especially in the south–western Cape. It was probably introduced accidentally in contaminated feed grain.

Brome is found in disturbed soil throughout the southern and western Cape and is now a major weed of wheat in the Sandveld and Swartland areas. Wheat monoculture and reduced tillage systems have encouraged this weed.

The species has hybridised with a close relative creating what is referred to as an 'aggregate' of very similar forms that are far more widespread and almost identical in appearance. The seedlings can be identified by their distinctive striped leaf sheaths. The leaves are also more hairy than those of the other common grass weeds of wheat in the Cape.

When mature, this grass is avoided by stock as the long barbed awns get into their nostrils and mouths. The spikes also contaminate clothing and sheep's wool. Brome can be a competitive weed, and is a host for cereal root diseases. Contaminated grain also blocks grading screens.

B. pectinatus is a similar species, also thought to be from Eurasia.

Control is especially difficult in wheat as ripgut brome is not susceptible to the selective grass killers normally used to control wild oats and other grasses. Suppression can be achieved with winter fallow ploughing, using a plough in seedbed preparation to bury the seed deeply. A suitable crop rotation such as lupins, medics, faba beans, canol or lucerne in which the cyclohexenone grass killers such as cycloxydim, fluazifop-p-butyl and quizalofop-p-ethyl can be used, is also recommended. If wheat is grown on wheat, sowing can be delayed until after the first rains have caused mass germination of seedlings. Reseedlings can then be destroyed with non-selective herbicides or tilling. It should be borne in mind, however, that not all the seeds germinate at the same time. Stubble burning in April also assists in suppressing this grass.

Bromus diandrus

POACEAE

Cenchrus brownii
Burgrass, Knopklitsgras

Cenchrus incertus
Mat sandbur, Dubbeltjiegras

Height: 20 cm

Introduced from tropical America, *C. brownii* and *C. incertus* are troublesome and unpleasant annual weeds occurring in many parts of South Africa.

C. brownii was introduced at about 1945. It is thought to have arrived on a tramp steamer which was harboured at the Bluff, Durban, and was first seen in nearby oil installations. Realising the potential danger, the authorities proclaimed it a weed in 1946 and formed a Burgrass Eradication Committee, which soon had the main infestation under control. However, by 1957 the weed had spread along the Natal South Coast and to several sites further inland.

C. incertus is more widespread than *C. brownii*, and is found in all provinces. Its route of introduction, however, is uncertain.

Both these weeds are usually found in such places as disturbed veld, waste areas and fallow land. They are only occasionally found in crop land.

They differ from each other in that the burs of *C. incertus* do not have fine outer bristles and that the inner ones do not bend inwards. These burs, especially the more robust ones of *C. incertus* can injure the feet and mouths of grazing animals. They can also stick to clothing and contaminate sheep's wool.

These two species of *Cenchrus* are not controlled effectively by pre–emergence herbicides. Effective control is achieved by post–emergence herbicides or cultivation whilst they are seedlings.

POACEAE

Cenchrus cillaris
Blue buffalo grass, Bloubuffelgras

Height: 60 cm

Blue buffalo grass is an indigenous, perennial grass. It has light, fluffy seeds as opposed to the burs of the other *Cenchrus* species.

It is common and widespread in South Africa, growing well in sandy or stony soils. This grass can be an excellent source of grazing in areas of low rainfall or in times of drought. It can, however, become a nuisance along roadsides, for example, where it may need to be controlled to improve visibility, tidiness, reduce the fire hazard etc.

No herbicides have been registered to control this grass.

Cenchrus incertus

Cenchrus cillaris

35

POACEAE

Chloris gayana
Rhodes grass, Rhodesgras

Chloris pycnothrix
Spiderweb chloris, Spinnerak-chloris

Chloris virgata
Feathertop chloris, Witpluim-chloris

Height: 0,5 – 2 m

These three species of *Chloris* are thought to be indigenous.

C. gayana is a tall, tufted, stoloniferous perennial grass common on roadsides and disturbed soil in general, but favouring the shade under trees and bushes. Originally recommended as a pasture grass by Cecil Rhodes, it has now lost much of its popularity mainly due to its lack of persistence. The plant's inflorescence of up to 20 spikes is quite distinctive. The origin of Rhodes grass is uncertain. Even though it is indigenous to Central Africa, there is a possibility that early introductions into South Africa were made from India.

C. pycnothrix is similar to *C. gayana*, but less widespread and smaller (up to 500 mm tall). It is recognizable by the rounded tips of the leaves. It is an annual and occurs mainly on road verges.

C. virgata is a widespread grass but it is only a serious arable problem in parts of the western O.F.S. and western Transvaal. It can behave as a perennial but, when weedy, acts as an annual. It is also a weed in overgrazed veld in the southern O.F.S. and Karoo. Stems can vary in height from only a few centimetres up to 90 cm – even on the same plant. Roots may develop from the lower nodes where they touch the ground. Feathertop chloris is easily identified by its characteristic, feathery, white spikes in the inflorescence. The spikes in each inflorescence vary from four to fifteen but are usually closer to four. The Xhosa use a decoction of this grass or its root in a bath for the treatment of colds and rheumatism.

These species are relatively easy to control by cultivation during the seedling stages and with pre-emergence grass herbicides of which several have been registered.

POACEAE

Cynodon dactylon
Quickgrass, Couch grass, Kweek, Kweekgras, Ngwengwe (Zulu)

Height: 30 cm

Thought to have originated in tropical Africa or Asia this grass is now a widespread and troublesome weed. It is considered to be the most widely distributed grass weed in the world. In South Africa its widespread and troublesome nature is demonstrated

36

Chloris gayana

Chloris pycnothrix

Chloris virgata

Cynodon dactylon

37

by the fact that it has 65 English and Afrikaans names as well as 14 recorded names in the various black languages.

Couch grass is a creeping perennial and is spread by means of an extensive system of stolons and underground rhizomes. It also disperses on animal hooves and cultivator tines. It does not grow very tall, with the flowering stem rarely reaching 40 cm. This stem produces a whorl of up to 10 fingers, one whorl to each stem. The flower produces viable seed.

C. dactylon is a vigorous grower and is capable of breaking up tarred or concrete surfaces. Its tough growth habit, however, also makes it a valuable grass for combating erosion. Several cultivars, mainly narrow–leaved ones have been developed for use in lawns, golf greens and sports fields.

Because of its extensive underground system, this weed is extremely difficult to eradicate. Repeated winter ploughing and harrowing will give a fair degree of control by breaking up the runners and exposing them to the elements. This reduces root reserves and increases the efficiency of the systemic post-emergence grass killers when they are applied to the regrowth. Although this weed is not susceptible to most pre–emergence herbicides, it can be controlled pre-emergent on roadsides and in industrial situations, with some industrial herbicides.

POACEAE

Cyndon nlemfuensis
Star grass, Stergras

Height: 1 m

Star grass was introduced from Kenya in 1919. It is now naturalised in parts of the warmer areas of South Africa, especially the Natal coastal regions and the northern and eastern Transvaal.

It occurs as a weed in patches in open and dense bushveld, cattle kraals, on roadsides, as well as in orchards and agricultural land, particularly in moist places.

Star grass is a vigorous grower, palatable and nutritious. It is planted for pasture and used for hay but once established, easily spreads into other areas were it becomes a nuisance.

Star grass is a perennial plant with a strong system of stolons. It is therefore extremely difficult to control. If one attempts to remove the plant mechanically it just tends to break up the runners and spread them around. Systemic herbicides can be used, but the grass should first be mowed or heavily grazed and even watered and fertilized. This will encourage fresh, green growth that is more capable of absorbing and translocating a herbicide.

Cyndon nlemfuensis

POACEAE

Dactylis glomerata
Cocksfoot, Koksvoetgras

Height: 80 cm

Introduced into South Africa from Europe for use as a fodder crop, this grass has escaped into the wild and is now widespread.

It is a perennial grass reproducing only by means of seeds.

Cocksfoot can often be found growing in shade and in disturbed areas such as roadsides especially where water accumulates, even though it does not tolerate waterlogging. A large number of varieties of cocksfoot are available commercially. They however, vary in their flowering date, leafiness and seasonal spread of foliar production. The plants are frost tolerant and are used as winter pastures in much the same way as ryegrass.

Cocksfoot is probably only a commercial problem on roadsides where it is easily controlled by industrial herbicides.

POACEAE

Dactyloctenium aegyptium
Crowfoot(grass), Coast(duck)grass, Hoenderspoor

Dactyloctenium australe
L.M. grass, Natalkweek

Dactyloctenium giganteum
Giant crowfoot, Reusehoenderspoor

Height: 10 – 40 cm

Crowfoot, being of uncertain origin but probably exotic, is an annual spreading grass. It is found mainly in the summer rainfall areas of South Africa, both in the temperate areas and subtropical regions, but is more common in the latter region. It spreads by means of stem-suckers formed where nodes on the stem touch the ground and take root. The plant produces an abundance of seed.

It is found along roadsides and in waste places and is frequently a pest in sub-tropical fruit orchards.

D. australe is indigenous, not as weedy as D. aegyptium and only common in the warmer sub-tropical areas of South Africa. It is a perennial and a popular lawn grass as it can spread vigorously by means of above-ground stolons.

D. giganteum is indigenous and widespread in the sub-tropical parts of the summer rainfall region.

Although crowfoot can be a strong competitor, it can be controlled effectively by conventional grass herbicides and shallow cultivation.

Dactylis glomerata

Dactyloctenium giganteum

Dactyloctenium aegyptium

41

POACEAE

Digitaria sanguinalis
Crab finger-grass, Kruisvingergras, Kruisgras

Height: 60 cm

Crab finger-grass is of uncertain origin, but it was probably introduced from Europe.

It is a major weed of crops and gardens in most areas, particularly the Natal Midlands, the Transvaal Highveld and the Eastern Cape.

It has a relatively flattened growth habit, growing to only about 0,6 m high, and can put down roots from nodes when they touch the ground. The number of 'fingers' varies from five to ten.

Often referred to by farmers as one of the four "landsgrasses", along with *Eleusine coracana*, *Urochloa panicoides*, and *Panicum schinzii* because they are common and as seedlings, appear similar. There are also several other very similar, closely related species of *Digitaria*.

Crab finger-grass is a serious problem in maize, where it competes vigorously for available moisture, especially later in the season. Fortunately, it is controlled effectively by the acetanelide group of herbicides. Prior to the introduction of these chemicals, however, this weed was increasing in importance as it did not respond well to thiocarbamates like EPTC. The seeds only germinate in soil temperatures exceeding 34°C. This means that in most of the maize producing areas, plants emerge late in early planted crops. For this reason chemicals with a long residual action are required. It is often advantageous to use a 'split application' of a pre–emergence residual grass herbicide, using some early and saving the rest for a later application when temperatures have become warmer.

POACEAE

Echinochloa colona
Marsh grass, Jungle rice, Moerasgras, Kleinwatergras

Echinochloa crus-galli
Barnyard grass, Barnyard millet, Hanepootmanna, Tuinmanna, Blousaadgras

Height: 1,5 m

E. colona is probably indigenous whereas *E. crus-galli* is thought to be from Eurasia. They are reported to be weeds of more than 35 crops in over 60 countries worldwide.

Despite their different origins, these annual grasses are very similar in appearance. *E. crus-galli* tends to have a more purple coloration and the awns on the seeds are longer than that of *E. colona*.

They are both widespread and common, favouring moist places and often grow in standing water. They are therefore weeds of ditches and irrigated crops, especially

Digitaria sanguinalis

Echinochloa colona

Echinochloa crus-galli

rice. *E. crus-galli* in particular is often a serious problem in irrigated crops.

Barnyard grass is sometimes planted as a forage crop as it can produce a heavy crop in 6 – 8 weeks. It therefore has value as a summer catch crop. It can grow up to 2 m in height and is a strong competitor.

Marsh grass is of less economic importance, preferring even moister conditions than barnyard grass. It is commonly found in gardens, on roadsides and in waste places. It is a weed of rice in areas where this crop is grown.

These grasses are controlled effectively by shallow cultivation and conventional pre- or post-emergence grass herbicides.

POACEAE

Ehrharta longiflora
Oat-seed grass, Hawersaadgras

Height: 1 m

There are over thirty indigenous species of *Ehrharta*. Several of them are considered weedy, although they are of relatively minor importance.

Oat-seed grass is an annual and like most of the family, is found mainly in the southern Cape regions. It occurs in disturbed areas such as roadsides and orchards and can become dense and competitive. It must not be confused with any of the wild oat species. These grasses often grow together, especially on roadsides.

It can be controlled by shallow cultivation during the seedling stage and is susceptible to pre- and post-emergence herbicides registered for use in orchards.

POACEAE

Eleusine coracana subsp. africana (=E. indica subsp. africana/E. africana)
African goosegrass, Rapoko grass, Afrikaanse osgras, Jongosgras

Eleusine indica subsp. indica
Indian goosegrass, Oxgrass, Indiese Osgras, Osgras

Height: 70 cm

Eleusine coracana subsp. *africana* is a widespread and troublesome annual grass weed of crops and gardens. It is probably indigenous and is considered by some authorities to be the most common grass weed of cultivated land in South Africa.

Eleusine indica subsp. *indica* is probably exotic and confined to the coastal districts of Natal and Zululand. Both species are almost identical with distinctive flattened stems which, unlike that of most grasses, are green.

Ehrharta longiflora

Eleusine coracana subsp. africana

Goosegrass is often referred to by farmers as one of the four "landsgrasses", along with *Digitaria sanguinalis*, *Urochloa panicoides*, and *Panicum schinzii*. These grasses are common and plentiful grass weeds of crop lands. As seedlings the four species look very similar.

Goosegrass is difficult to pull up by hand because of its strong roots. It is also not easy to cut in lawns because of its tough stems. It is not a very palatable grazing grass, but in times of famine the seed is ground into flour and eaten.

Goosegrass will continue to germinate throughout the summer season, therefore cultivation is not an efficient method of control. Fortunately it is very susceptible to the grass herbicides and even to some pre-emergence so-called 'broadleaf-weed' herbicides. However, because of its highly competitive nature, the use of specialised grass killers is often essential.

POACEAE

Eragrostis cilianensis
Stinking eragrostis, Stink love grass, Stink-eragrostis, Stinkgras

Eragrostis curvula
Weeping love grass, Oulandsgras

Eragrostis plana
Fan love grass, Taaipol-eragrostis

Eragrostis pseudosclerantha
Footpath love grass, Voetpad eragrostis

Eragrostis racemosa
Narrow heart love grass, Smalhartjie-eragrostis

Eragrostis superba
Heart seed love grass, Weeluis-eragrostis

Eragrostis trichophora
Hairy love grass, Blousaad

Height: 1,5 m

These seven species of *Eragrostis* are representatives of a large group (genus) of indigenous grasses that include both weeds and valuable pasture grasses.

E. curvula is used as a hay crop and in permanent pastures. It is versatile and widely distributed. Unfortunately it is a problem as a volunteer as it invades some perennial crops.

E. cilianensis is also a common weed but is seldom a problem in agronomic crops. It is, however, aromatic and although said to be unpalatable, will contaminate the milk of cows if they consume it.

Eragrostis curvula

Eragrostis pseudosclerantha

Eragrostis superba

Eragrostis trichophora

47

The Zulus and farmers refer to 'mtshiki', which is either veld with *E. plana*, *E. curvula*, *Sporobolus africanus* and *S. pyramidalis* occurring as a stand of similar upright grasses, or sometimes *E. plana* on its own. They are all pioneering in nature.

E. pseudoscleranthia, *E. racemosa*, *E. superba* and *E. trichophora* are weeds of roadsides and waste places.

These grasses are controlled effectively by pre–emergence grass killers. Post–emergence herbicides are generally less effective, especially once the grass is beyond the seedling stage or once it has tillered.

POACEAE

Hemarthria altissima
Red swamp grass, Rooikweek

Height: 1 m

Red swamp grass is an indigenous, perennial grass found throughout southern Africa. It has creeping underground rhizomes, stems which are usually red and an inflorescence which is often difficult to recognise as it looks like a continuation of the stem.

It is a palatable species and can be a useful fodder plant in the wet areas in which it grows. It can also be useful for binding soils in areas of potential erosion. Notwithstanding this, red swamp grass is a weed of roadsides and ditches. It may often need to be controlled or eradicated in order to prevent clogging in waterways or ditches.

Systemic or industrial herbicides would normally be required for successful control.

POACEAE

Heteropogon contortus
Common spear grass, Tanglehead, Gewone pylgras, Assegaaigras

Height: 1 m

An indigenous grass that is widespread in South Africa except in the west. It is not usually a competitive weed, although it does frequently occur in crop lands. It is most commonly found along roadsides, especially in bushveld areas.

It can cause considerable damage to livestock, however. The hygroscopic awns unwind in the presence of moisture and the barbed seeds can penetrate the skin of animals, sometimes causing infection. This invariably reduces the value of the skins. These seeds also cause discomfort to any person who happens to walk through veld where this grass occurs.

Common spear grass should be controlled when small.

Hemarthria altissima

Heteropogon contortus

POACEAE

Hordeum murinum
Wild barley, False barley, Mouse barley, Wildegars, Muiswildegars

Height: 20 cm

Of European origin, this grass is now an annual weed causing serious problems in parts of the southern and south-western Cape. It is only rarely seen outside of these areas.

Wild barley is commonly found on roadsides, in gardens, waste places and in crop lands, especially on headlands in wheat fields that have been cultivated but not planted. It is frequently found growing in lucerne where it is cut and eaten by livestock along with the lucerne. The sharp awns of wild barley can cause ulceration of the mucous membranes of the animals mouths. Apparently the mouths of horses are particularly sensitive to this grass. Ostriches can die from its effects.

Wild barley is controlled effectively by the selective post-emergence herbicides registered for use in lucerne.

POACEAE

Hyparrhenia hirta
Common thatching grass, Dekgras

Hyparrhenia tamba
Blue thatching grass, Bloutamboekiegras

Height: 1,5 – 2 m

There are many species of *Hyparrhenia* in South Africa. All of them are indigenous, perennial and collectively referred to as thatching grass.

Although representatives of this family can be found throughout the country in a wide range of sites they are especially common on roadsides.

Although these grasses are widely used for thatching purposes, they become a nuisance on roadsides as they are relatively tall, thereby obstructing visibility.

Several industrial herbicides have been registered for use where these grasses need to be controlled on roadsides and in industrial areas.

Hordeum murinum

Hyparrhenia tamba

POACEAE

Imperata cylindrica
Silver spike, Cotton wool grass, Silweraargras, Beddinggras, Donsgras

Height: 80 cm

This indigenous grass is a weed of many regions of the world and is said to be one of the most troublesome grass weeds of some of the tropical countries.

Silver spike occurs in moist places throughout South Africa, tending to take over once it has established itself. It is an unpalatable climax species and is often a serious problem on roadsides and in industrial areas. It is a spreading perennial grass with a system of underground rhizomes which makes it very difficult to control. However, silver spike can sometimes be of value in vleis and eroded watercourses as it may be the only plant able to survive the water–logged conditions and act as a soil binder, thus preventing erosion.

This grass is a potential problem in tropical plantation crops such as coffee.

When this weed occurs on roadsides and in industrial areas, it is of considerable economic importance, requiring the use of expensive systemic weed-killers or non-selective industrial herbicides.

POACEAE

Lagurus ovatus
Hare's tail(grass), Haasstert(gras)

Height: 50 cm

Of Mediterranean origin, this annual grass is now a weed in parts of South Africa, mainly the southern Cape and, especially around Knysna. It is also found as far east as Port Elizabeth and has even been recorded in Pretoria.

Hare's tail is found on roadsides, in waste places and in gardens and is used for ornamental purposes such as in flower arrangements.

No specific control measures are recommended for this weed, but it is easily removed by cultivation.

POACEAE

Leersia hexandra
Wild ricegrass, Wilderysgras

Height: 75 cm

An indigenous, perennial grass found throughout southern Africa. It has little agricultural significance as it usually grows in moist, shaded areas such as ditches and stream banks. Wild ricegrass is a problem, however, in drainage ditches and irrigation chan-

Imperata cylindrica

Lagurus ovatus

Leersia hexandra

53

nels, actually growing in the water, obstructing the channel, increasing stagnancy and breeding sites for mosquitoes and bilharzia–carrying snails.

Control is difficult on account of its strong underground system of rhizomes and would be best achieved with non–selective, systemic chemicals that can be applied near irrigation water.

POACEAE

Lolium multiflorum
Italian ryegrass, Annual ryegrass, Italiaanse raaigras

Lolium perenne
Perennial ryegrass, Meerjarige raaigras

Lolium temulentum
Darnel(ryegrass), Drabok(raaigras)

Height: 1 m

These closely related species from Europe are difficult to tell apart even for botanists, and are now naturalised throughout South Africa.

Annual ryegrass is usually shorter, has shiny leaves and the spikelets on the florets are absent. Darnel has shorter spikelets than Italian ryegrass and the florets are not as plump. The ryegrasses have been hybridised and bred as high performing pasture grasses, but often escape into the wild and become troublesome volunteer weeds.

Annual ryegrass can become infested with the nematode *Anguina agrostis* and a bacterium, *Corynebacterium rathayi* which together can cause fatal poisoning of livestock. This has been identified as the cause of heavy stock losses on several farms in the Ceres, Caledon and Bredasdorp districts since 1979. The first danger sign that the ryegrass is infected, is the presence of a yellow bacterial slime, usually occurring on the inflorescences in September.

Darnel is a wild-type and was probably introduced by early settlers as a contaminant of grain seed. It was the first weed to receive official attention, as in 1659, it became the subject of a 'plakkart' or regulation posted in public places by Van Riebeeck's council. It is now widespread in South Africa in cultivated lands, gardens and other disturbed places. When the seed is milled with wheat it is said to cause the flour to become grey, bitter and even poisonous. The grain is often infected with the fungus *Endoconidium temulentum* which causes the release of a toxin called 'loline' or 'temuline'. This toxin is said to be very dangerous to livestock and humans. Darnel also forms hybrids with the other species.

The ryegrasses are difficult to control when they occur in cereal crops. They are sensitive, however, to most of the selective grass and wild oats herbicides, even if it seems that there is some variation in herbicide sensitivity between the different species and varieties. Where practicable, they can easily be removed by cultivation during the seedling stage.

Lolium multiflorum

POACEAE

Melinis repens (=*Rhynchelytrum repens*)
Natal red-top, Natalse rooipluim

Height: 1 m

Although the name of this weed suggests that it is restricted to Natal, it is widely distributed throughout South Africa and indeed, the world. In fact, it is possibly not even indigenous as its origin is uncertain.

Natal red-top is a common annual or short lived perennial weed of such places as roadsides and waste places. It is capable of invading fallow lands but is seldom common in natural veld. It reproduces only by means of seeds, but frequently takes root at the lower nodes. Animals do not find it palatable, but it does provide cover in disturbed areas, thereby reducing erosion.

Shallow cultivation will control Natal red–top in the seedling stage and it is susceptible to many pre–emergence grass herbicides. On roadsides it is controlled effectively by conventional industrial herbicides.

POACEAE

Nassella neesiana (=*Stipa neesiana*)
Spear grass, Pylgras

Nassella tenuissima (=*Stipa tenuissima*)
White tussock, Witpolgras

Nassella trichotoma (=*Stipa trichotoma*)
Nassella tussock, Nassella-polgras

Height: 75 cm

These species of *Nassella* which are serious perennial weeds in South Africa, all originate in South America. (The *Nassella* genus has recently been separated from *Stipa*).

N. neesiana is found in the Eastern Cape and southern Natal. *N. tenuissima* occurs mainly around Barkley East near an infestation of *N. trichotoma*. This suggests a common origin which is thought to have been 130 000 tons of fodder brought into Port Elizabeth and East London for military purposes during the Anglo-Boer War. *N. trichotoma*, although more widespread, is still restricted mainly to the eastern Cape. It has, however, also been found at the Rhodes memorial in Cape Town and near Stellenbosch and Swellendam. Nassella tussock is a major weed in Australia and New Zealand. Where it occurs it is a very serious problem, rapidly invading veld and old lands which are in poor condition. Once this grass has become established it forms dense stands, totally displacing the naturally occurring species. On account of its unpalatability, the carrying capacity of the veld is drastically reduced.

Melinis repens

Nassella neesiana

Nassella trichotoma

57

Before flowering, which occurs from November to December, sheep and cattle will graze this grass, but after it has flowered the animals will not touch it. At maturity the whole inflorescence breaks off and blows away. At the peak of the invasion during the 1960s, these blowing inflorescences formed large drifts against fences. The long awns on the seeds of all four species adhere to clothing and hair which is a further very efficient means of dispersal.

Nassella tussock is a declared weed with the potential to force farmers off their land and jeopardise the economy of the country if it is not contained. The major infestations of the 1960s have been brought under control by means of an intensive and subsidised control programme initiated during 1976. However, the plant has not been totally eradicated and if the restraints of such a control programme are removed, this weed can easily become one of major importance once again. Thirty-six percent of South Africa is a suitable habitat for this grass.

Tetrapion is registered for the selective control of Nassella tussock seedlings. Glyphosate and proprop are also registered, but effective long-term eradication requires a comprehensive programme of chemical or physical removal over many years. Effective follow-ups and over–sowing of suitable grasses will also be necessary. Any infestation of Nassella tussock should be reported to the authorities so that advice can be given and proper control measures be rapidly taken.

POACEAE

Panicum maximum
Common Buffalo grass, Guinea grass, Gewone buffelsgras, Ubabe (Zulu), Lehola (Sotho)

Height: 2 m

This grass is a widespread and indigenous weed in South Africa. As it is the principal weed of sugar cane and many other crops, it is a source of great concern in agriculture.

Guinea grass is a vigorous grower and can develop large perennial clumps that can produce stems over 2 m tall. In extreme cases, stems of up to 4 m have been recorded. The leaves and stems are hairy, unlike that of *P. schinzii* (sweet buffalo grass) with which it can be confused, and it does not usually exhibit such strong purple colouration.

As it is a palatable plant some varieties have been selected and bred for commercial use as pasture grasses. In the warmer areas the plant is much more robust, often reaching 2, or 3 m in height. In the Cape, for instance, it is usually only about 1,5 m tall.

The seedlings are very weak and slow-growing and high mortality rates are experienced during drought periods. It is important to control this grass early, as plants that are not controlled at an early stage, develop large perennial clumps or 'stools'. These clumps are tolerant of even the strongest herbicides and must usually be removed by hand.

Panicum maximum

Seedlings are susceptible to conventional pre-emergence grass killers and easily controlled by post-emergence chemicals or shallow cultivation. Care must be taken to remove all late-germinating individuals as escaped plants become very competitive.

POACEAE

Panicum schinzii (=*Panicum laevifolium*)
Sweet buffalo grass, Vlei-panicum, Blue panic, Soetgras, Vleibuffelsgras, Blousaad(buffelsgras)

Height: 1 – 2 m

P. schinzii is a widespread and indigenous annual grass weed, especially in the cooler and/or moister areas. It can grow to 2 m, with hollow stems that are usually purple or red. The stems are hairless, except at the ligule. This characteristic makes it easy to differentiate from *P. maximum* (Guinea grass).

Sweet buffalo grass is a common weed of crops and gardens in most areas. In the high rainfall regions it is often the dominant grass weed.

It is a highly palatable grass and excellent for hay or silage although its high moisture content and thick hollow stems make it rather difficult to make into hay, especially in the summer rainfall areas. Being an annual, unlike *Eragrostis* for example, it does not produce regrowth after cutting.

Buffalo grass competes vigorously for moisture in crops such as maize. It is one of the four species commonly referred to as "landsgrasses" because their seedlings are similar and they occur frequently. The others are: *Digitaria sanguinalis, Eleusine coracana,* and *Urochloa panicoides.*

Buffalo grass is susceptible to conventional pre-emergence grass herbicides. At a young stage they can be killed with certain post-emergence chemicals and by means of shallow cultivation.

POACEAE

Paspalum distichum (=*P. paspalodes*)
Paspalum, Buffalo quick paspalum, Couch paspalum, Buffelskweekpaspalum, Kweekpaspalum

Paspalum notatum
Lawn paspalum, Bahia paspalum, Turfpaspalum, Bahiagras

Height: 50 cm

P. distichum is thought by some authorities to be indigenous, but by others to be a native of South America.

Paspalum is a widespread perennial weed in South Africa, distributed in moist sites

Panicum schinzii

Paspalum notatum

such as waterways, drainage channels and in moister crop lands. The flowers are light green, often with contrasting black female parts (stigmas). Despite favouring moister areas, paspalum can withstand drought conditions for a reasonable period. It is however, a palatable species on which sheep may do well in winter provided they are able to get to the succulent underground stolons which remain nutritious, even after frost has occurred.

This weed's underground system of creeping stems makes it very difficult to eradicate. Ploughing and discing merely tend to spread it. High rates of the systemic grass killers are required to control this weed successfully.

P. notatum, which is unanimously considered to be from South America, is an aggressive invader of lawns, but can often make a good surface for some kinds of sports fields. It generally does not require much cutting, but the flowering stems shoot up rapidly and make the turf unsightly if they are not trimmed frequently.

Lawn paspalum also has a system of underground rhizomes which necessitates the use of systemic herbicides for effective control.

POACEAE

Paspalum dilatatum
Common paspalum, Gewone paspalum

Paspalum urvillei
Tall paspalum, Giant paspalum, Langbeenpaspalum

Height: 1 – 2 m

These two exotic species of grass from South America are widespread weeds in South Africa, being particularly well-known to sugarcane and pineapple growers.

P. dilatatum is a perennial, being spread by seeds or rhizomes, and is especially difficult to control once established. It is an important weed of fruit orchards, often interfering with micro-irrigation systems. Although it should be controlled before it becomes established it is susceptible to the systemic grass killers.

P. urvillei only reproduces by seed but can grow into a large, tufted, perennial clump which is tolerant to many herbicides. It is a major weed of forestry and pineapples, but is also common in waste places, along roadsides and moist areas in general. It is palatable and nutritious and in the right place, a useful pasture grass. *P. urvillei* is taller, with a more erect growth habit than *P. dilatatum*.

Again, control of tall paspalum should be implemented early as it is difficult to control once mature. When young and growing vigorously, it can be controlled by the systemic grass killers and some industrial herbicides. Before germination it is susceptible to the conventional pre-emergence grass herbicides.

Paspalum dilatatum

Paspalum urvillei

POACEAE

Pennisetum clandestinum
Kikuyu, Kikoejoe

Pennisetum setaceum
Fountain grass, Pronkgras

Pennisetum villosum
Feathertop, Haarwurmgras

Height: 50 cm

Introduced from East Africa, kikuyu is now widely distributed in the summer rainfall regions, both as a cultivated plant and where it has escaped, as a weed. It is a robust, perennial, creeping plant and a valuable summer grazing grass widely used in lawns and sports turfs.

The fine threadlike anthers on a kikuyu sward are a common sight, but the local strains have always produced little or no seed. (This made pasture establishment difficult. At the same time, however, it also reduced the likelihood of escape.) The advent of seeding varieties may make this grass more troublesome as a weed.

Kikuyu is particularly sensitive to glyphosate which can be used for its general as well as for its selective control in *Cynodon* turf. Otherwise, as this grass is frost–sensitive, winter ploughing and discing gives a fair degree of suppression. It should be borne in mind though, that any remaining runners, under suitable conditions, will spread rapidly. Kikuyu is not susceptible to pre-emergence herbicides.

P. setaceum and *P. villosum* were both introduced from North Africa as ornamentals and have escaped into the wild. They are now common perennial weeds of roadsides and waste places.

Once established they become difficult to control.

POACEAE

Perotis patens
Purple spike cat's tail, Bottlebrush grass, Persaar-katstertgras

Height: 0,5 m

An indigenous grass that can be either an annual or a perennial, reproducing only by means of seeds.

This grass is typically found on poorer, sandy soils in the warmer areas, such as in citrus orchards. Because of its pioneering nature it will invade overgrazed veld and disturbed ground which is undesirable as this grass has very little grazing value.

No herbicides have been registered for this grass. It should, however, be susceptible to regular weed control programmes such as those employed in orchards.

Pennisetum villosum

Perotis patens

Pennisetum clandestinum

Pennisetum setaceum

65

POACEAE

Phalaris canariensis
Common canary grass, Gewone kanariegras

Phalaris minor
Little-seeded canary grass, Kleinsaadkanariegras

Height: 1 – 1,5 m

Introduced from the Mediterranean region, probably as a fodder crop, these annual grasses are now widespread in South Africa. They are particularly troublesome in cereals in the Cape Province.

The seedlings can be identified quite easily as they will exude a red juice from the stem and roots when broken. Although the two species are very similar in appearance, *P. minor* is somewhat smaller than *P. canariensis*.

These grasses are easy to control in cereals as they are susceptible to the highly effective range of selective grass herbicides registered for use in these crops.

(A very similar grass, *P. aquatica*, is a perennial and not as widespread. It is also from the European region but is usually only found on roadsides and in waste places.)

POACEAE

Poa annua
Annual bluegrass, Wintergrass, Eenjarige blougras, Wintergras

Height: 30 cm

This grass is a relatively small, bright green annual plant that is a native of Europe. It is now distributed worldwide and common in all areas of South Africa.

It grows throughout the year in damp and shady places and is particularly noticeable in winter. It can be a troublesome weed in gardens, lawns and golf courses and bowling greens where little green tufts remain when the cultivated grass has frosted off. It is also found near places such as leaking taps, where the soil may be too damp for other species.

During winter when golf courses or lawns for example, are brown and dormant, this weed can be controlled by means of non-selective contact herbicides. However, in the summer months selective post-emergence chemicals will be required.

Phalaris minor

Poa annua

POACEAE

Polypogon monspeliensis
Beard grass, Rabbit's foot, Brakbaardgras, Brakgras

Height: 40 cm

Originally from Europe and Asia this grass was probably introduced as an ornamental and is now naturalised in many parts of South Africa, especially coastal areas.

It grows well on 'brak' or brackish soils but despite its lush growth, it is not a good grazing species. It favours moist places.

Although it is an annual, rabbit's foot appears to be relatively tolerant to many herbicides. It is probably best controlled by shallow cultivation in the early stages. No herbicides have been registered for controlling this weed.

POACEAE

Rottboellia cochinchinensis (=R. *exaltata*)
Guinea-fowl grass, Shamva grass, Itch grass, Tarentaalgras

Height: 1 – 2 m

This is a major annual grass weed worldwide. It is a problem plant in several crops, especially sugar cane in the sub-tropical areas of the Philippines, Columbia, Cuba, the U.S.A. as well as in South Africa.

It is indigenous to Africa and has spread into many sugar cane growing areas in South Africa, particularly northern Zululand. It also occurs in maize at Normandien and Colenso in Natal and at various sites in the Transvaal, especially in the eastern Lowveld.

The stiff, sharp hairs on the basal leaf sheath of this grass are easily dislodged and cause skin irritations. For this reason, it is internationally known as itch grass.

Itch grass only grows from seeds which are large and mainly dispersed by water, wind and human activities. Guinea-fowl in particular, find them very palatable.

It is a deep–rooted grass and not selectively controlled by pre-emergence grass in sugar cane and maize. It is best controlled at the seedling stage with post-emergence herbicides or by cultivation.

Rottboellia cochinchinensis

Polypogon monspeliensis

POACEAE

Setaria megaphylla (=S. chevalieri)
Ribbon bristle grass, Broad-leaved setaria, Breëblaarborselgras, Breëblaarsetaria

Height: 2 m

S. megaphylla is an indigenous, large and robust perennial grass that is widespread in the eastern half of South Africa's summer rainfall region.

It favours moist and shady areas such as those under trees. As a problem weed it is best known in forestry where it is difficult to eradicate once it has become established. For this reason it is a major weed of silviculture. It is planted in gardens as an ornamental.

Ribbon bristle grass can be controlled in forestry with relatively high rates of systemic herbicides like glyphosate, but this is laborious and expensive on mature plants.

Control should be initiated when the plants are still small. Some foresters have had success eradicating the weed even before clear felling. This ensures that the rapid regrowth of this grass is prevented when the trees are removed.

POACEAE

Setaria nigrirostris
Large seed setaria, Grootsaadsetaria

Setaria pallide-fusca
Red bristle grass, Garden setaria, Rooiborselgras, Tuinsetaria, Perdesoetgras

Setaria sphacelata
Golden setaria, Common setaria, Goue setaria, Gewone setaria

Setaria verticillata
Sticky bristle grass, Klitsborselgras

Height: 1 – 2 m

There are many species of Setaria, the above-mentioned four being the most troublesome as weeds. (S. megaphylla is dealt with separately.) They are all probably indigenous.

S. nigrirostris is an occasional weed along roadsides and in waste places.

S. pallide-fusca is an annual agricultural weed causing serious problems in most areas of the summer rainfall region. As it often appears in maize late in the season, it escapes regular pre-emergence herbicides. It subsequently presents a fire hazard in winter. The plant's bright orange seed-heads make it stand out from other weeds. The seedlings of this grass are characterised by their upright growth habit and bright red stem bases.

Setaria megaphylla

Setaria sphacelata

Setaria pallide-fusca

Setaria verticillata

71

S. sphacelata is mainly found in the eastern half of the summer rainfall areas in moist sites, along watercourses, in ditches and along roadsides, especially in the mist belt. It is an extremely variable species and occurs in a number of forms and sub-species.

S. verticillata is an annual grass which is widely distributed in South Africa, except in Natal, where it is rare. It is common in gardens and other disturbed places, especially where it is damp or shaded. The bristles characteristically adhere to clothing or the hair of animals which is an efficient means of dispersal. It contaminates sheep's wool. In parts of Africa the seed-head is used to cover stored grain to keep rats off as their fur gets entangled in the barbed bristles.

S. pallide-fusca in particular, is controlled effectively by pre- and post-emergence herbicides when applied timeously. The other setaria grasses are also susceptible to herbicides and their seedlings are easily destroyed by cultivation.

POACEAE

Sorghum bicolor subsp. **arundinaceum** (=*S. verticilliflorum*)
Common wild sorghum, Gewone wildesorghum

Sorghum bicolor subsp. **drummondii** (=*S. almum*)
Wild grain sorghum, Wildegraansorghum

Sorghum halepense
Johnson grass, Johnsongras

Sorghum versicolor
Black seed wild sorghum, Swartsaadwildesorghum

Height: 2,5 m

This group of closely related grasses is causing serious problems in agriculture.

Sorghum bicolor subsp. *arundinaceum* is an indigenous grass. It reproduces only by means of seeds, but is capable of producing large perennial clumps. It is common throughout Natal and the Transvaal and is a particularly problematic weed in subtropical crops in the Natal coastal belt and the Transvaal Lowveld. In sugar cane for example, this grass can cause major problems. It can grow as tall as the cane and is difficult to locate because its broad leaves are very similar to that of the sugar cane. If allowed to establish itself, it can only be controlled effectively by hand.

Sorghum bicolor subsp. *drummondii* is an annual from elsewhere in Africa. It resembles grain sorghum and has only become a problem since the 1970s. Its distribution is centred around Lichtenburg in the western Transvaal and Bronkhorstspruit in the eastern Transvaal.

S. halepense, which was introduced from Europe, is perhaps potentially the most serious weed of these four species. It differs from the others by having rhizomes from which it can reproduce and grow large perennial 'stools'. At present though in South Africa, it is not as common as *S. bicolor* subsp. *arundinaceum* and is restricted mainly to the Transvaal.

72

Sorghum halepense

Sorghum bicolor subsp. arundinaceum

73

Sorghum versicolor is an indigenous annual grass, characterised by a hairy node, and an inflorescence that is partly black. Black seed wild sorghum prefers black turf soils in the Transvaal and northern Natal.

The pollen from these plants is known to cause hay fever and like all *Sorghum* species can cause prussic acid poisoning in animals.

As seedlings, these grasses are susceptible to pre- or early post-emergence grass herbicides. Effective control of these weeds depends on the timeous and efficient application of these herbicides. Once these grasses become established, they are extremely difficult to eradicate.

POACEAE

Sporobolus africanus
Rat's tail dropseed, Rotstertfynsaadgras, Mtshiki (Zulu)

Sporobolus fimbriatus
Common dropseed, Bushveld dropseed, Gewone fynsaadgras, Bosveldfynsaadgras

Sporobolus pyramidalis
Cat's tail dropseed, Katstertfynsaadgras

Height: 1,5 m

Dropseed are indigenous, perennial grasses that are members of the group referred to as 'mtshiki' by the Zulu and many farmers, because of their similar, upright growth habit. Other species in this group are *Eragrostis curvula* and *E. plana*.

S. africanus is the most common, being widespread in South Africa and found in disturbed ground and compacted areas. *S. fimbriatus* and *S. pyramidalis* are relatively less common, but also occur as weeds in disturbed or compacted areas. They are not usually weeds of annual crops.

Control of these grasses with herbicides is variable and usually the higher rates are recommended. They are probably most effectively controlled by cultivation when still in the seedling stage.

POACEAE

Stenotaphrum secundatum
St. Augustine grass, Coastal buffalo grass, Augustinuskweek, Strandbuffelsgras

Height: 40 cm

A creeping perennial grass of uncertain origin that is common in the coastal areas of southern Africa.

It is widely used in lawns on sandy soils where it forms a dense, rather coarse mat. It does not invade crops, but is usually found as a weed on roadsides and in waste places etc.

St. Augustine grass is controlled effectively by industrial and systemic grass killers.

74

Sporobolus africanus

Sporobolus pyramidalis

Stenotaphrum secundatum

POACEAE

Tragus berteronianus
Small carrot-seed grass, Kleinwortelsaadgras

Tragus racemosus
Large carrot-seed grass, Stalked carrot-seed grass, Grootwortelsaadgras, Losaar-
wortelsaadgrass

Height: 20 cm

These two closely related indigenous, annual species are similar in appearance and in
their distribution, which is widespread, except in the south-western Cape.

The main difference between the two carrot-seed grasses is that the spikelets of *T. race-
mosus* are longer and larger. It is difficult to identify them in the field unless they occur
together.

As weeds of crops, these grasses occur mainly in the Transvaal Lowveld and in
Northern Transvaal where they appear in many locations. Elsewhere these grasses
usually grow in sandy places, in waste areas and on roadsides, often in pure stands
and forming loose mats. They are prolific producers of viable seeds and therefore
spread rapidly. The hooked spikelets often cling to the wool of sheep and to clothing.

Both carrot-seed grasses are susceptible to normal pre- and post-emergence grass herbicides.

POACEAE

Urochloa mosambicensis
Bushveld herringbone grass, Bosveldbeesgras

Urochloa panicoides
Garden urochloa, Herringbone grass, Tuinurochloa, Beesgras

Height: 70 cm

U. panicoides is a common and often serious indigenous annual grass weed of most
crops in most areas, but usually on heavier soils. It is most common in the north-western Orange Free State, the western Transvaal and the eastern Transvaal highveld.

Herringbone grass is one of the four species of grasses commonly referred to as 'landsgrasses', because they are common and as seedlings, similar annual grass weeds of
crop lands. (The other 'landsgrasses' are *Digitaria sanguinalis, Eleusine coracana* and
Panicum schinzii).

Herringbone grass is easily identified from the other 'landsgrasses' by its crinkly leaf
margins and by being noticeably hairy. When established, it often roots from the lower
nodes.

Urochloa mosambicensis

Tragus berteronianus

Urochloa panicoides

77

As germination takes place over a short period in the spring, timely cultivation can give good control. Furthermore, *U. panicoides* is well controlled by most of the grass herbicides although it seems to be relatively tolerant to the triazines.

U. mosambicensis is similar in appearance to *U. panicoides*. It is indigenous and found in the warmer, eastern regions of South Africa. It is a perennial, but seldom occurs as such in cultivated lands as it grows readily from seed. This grass also invades veld and produces underground runners, especially under heavy grazing. It is, in fact, very palatable and in such instances, desirable.

Like *U. panicoides*, it is also very susceptible to the normal grass herbicides.

POACEAE

Vulpia myuros
Rat's tail fescue, Langbaardswenkgras, Wildegars

Height: 25 cm

Introduced from Europe, this is now a serious annual grass weed in the southern regions of South Africa.

Although *V. myuros* is restricted mainly to the southern and eastern Cape, it is common in these areas. *V. bromoides*, a very similar species, can be found as far north as Natal, where it tends to favour comparatively drier areas.

Rat's tail fescue is a common weed of roadsides, waste places and gardens, especially in lawns, and in lucerne.

This weed is difficult to control once it has become established and does not respond to most selective grass killers. Control should be initiated when the plants are small.

CYPERACEAE

Bulbostylis hispidula (=Fimbristylis hispidula)
Slender sedge, Fynbiessie

Height: 20 cm

Quite a common and indigenous weed, but very rarely a problem, although it is frequently found growing in crops.

It is easy to distinguish between the slender sedge and the nutsedges by looking at its much finer leaves. The slender sedge is common on sandy soils. It is relatively unpalatable and is therefore undesirable in pastures.

Slender sedge is susceptible to cultivation and many herbicides.

Vulpia myuros

Bulbostylis hispidula

CYPERACEAE

Cyperus esculentus
Yellow nutsedge, Yellow nut-grass, Geeluintjie

Height: 35 cm

Although sometimes mistakenly referred to as a grass, this weed is not a grass, but a sedge. It is of uncertain origin, but it is thought that it could be exotic. In America it is called 'Northern nutsedge', as it tends to grow in the cooler northern areas as opposed to the 'Southern nutsedge' (*C. rotundus*), with which it is easily confused. In South Africa this trend is repeated with *C. esculentus* being widespread in the cooler areas, and *C. rotundus* occurring in the subtropical areas and warmer valleys. They frequently occur together and are further confused with about 90 indigenous species of *Cyperus*.

Yellow nutsedge reproduces from tubers or 'nuts' that are produced in vast numbers underground at the ends of the rhizomes. One tuber can produce 1900 plants and in turn nearly 7 000 tubers, covering an area of 2 m² in one year. The tubers are edible, with a faint nutty taste, (unlike the bitter taste of *C. rotundus*). They are easily washed to new areas by storm water. The plant can also reproduce from shallow germinating seeds which will spread it further afield.

The rhizomes, which are chewed by the Zulus as a cure for indigestion, can cause serious damage to crops such as potatoes. They are able to grow right through a developing potato and nuts are often found inside the potato tuber.

The nutsedges are serious and competitive weeds, not only because they are widespread, difficult to control and aggressive, but also because they can release a toxin that can suppress the growth of other plants. This phenomenon is known as 'allelopathy'.

Of the two 'uintjie' species, the yellow nutsedge is easier to control as it is susceptible to the acetanelides, bendioxide and thiocarbamates like EPTC. However, specific conditions are required for these chemicals to be effective. Successful control can reduce the population in the following year by 90%.

Mechanical control is usually not very effective as the tubers are not easily killed by desiccation.

CYPERACEAE

Cyperus rotundus
Purple nutsedge, Purple nut-grass, Red nut-grass, Rooi-uintjie

Height: 20 cm

Purple nutsedge is not as widespread as yellow nutsedge, being confined to the warmer frost–free areas. It is a major weed worldwide having been recorded as a weed in 52 crops in 92 countries. However, it is much more difficult to control as it resists most selective herbicides except thiocarbamates like EPTC as well as MSMA. It is

Cyperus rotundus

Cyperus esculentus

therefore very important to be able to identify the nutsedges before expensive control programmes are initiated.

Like *C. esculentus*, it produces massive numbers of nuts or tubers, (up to 8 700 per m²), but unlike *C. esculentus*, it can only produce a few viable seeds. These generally germinate shallowly but in extreme cases can germinate from depths as great as 30 cm.

Tubers of purple nutsedge are more likely to be killed by desiccation and exposure than those of yellow nutsedge.

The following are the main differences between yellow and red nutsedge:

	Cyperus esculentus Yellow nutsedge	*Cyperus rotundus* Purple nutsedge
Leaf colour	pale	darker
Growth habit	usually erect	tending to be squatter
Height	30 – 40 cm average	10 – 20 cm average
Stems	no hard lump	hard lump at base
Leaf shape	tapered	pointed
Nuts	round	irregular
	ends of rhizomes	in strings
	nutty taste	bitter
Distribution	everywhere	warmer areas
Herbicides (selective)	acetanelides	EPTC
	bendioxide	MSMA
	EPTC	
	MSMA	
Desiccation	less effective	more effective

CYPERACEAE

Kyllinga alba
White sedge, Witbiesie

Kyllinga erecta
White kyllinga, Witbiesie

Height: 40 cm

These are indigenous sedges which are occasionally a problem in lawns, sports turfs, waste areas, forestry and orchards throughout the country. They are known to become

Kyllinga erecta

dense and troublesome in orchards in the Eastern Transvaal.

These sedges propagate from underground rhizomes which makes them tolerant to contact herbicides.

ALLIACEAE

Nothoscordum gracile
Fragrant false–garlic, Onion weed, Basterknoffel

Height : 0,5 m

A native of North America that is now widespread. In South Africa it is a common weed of nurseries and gardens.

Fragrant false garlic resembles an onion or garlic but without the smell. This plant regenerates from underground bulbs as well as seeds.

Mainly because of its waxy leaves and underground bulbs, it is not susceptible to herbicides and none have been registered. It is best removed by hand, and care should be taken that all the bulblets are removed.

ASPARAGACEAE

Protasparagus laricinus (=Asparagus laricinus)
Wild asparagus, Katbos

Height: 2 m

There are many indigenous species of wild asparagus occurring in all parts of South Africa and they often become troublesome weeds.

Some of the species of wild asparagus have spines, while many have white flowers and red berries. They are capable of forming impenetrable clumps along roads, fences and in waste places etc. Farmers in the north-western Free State in particular, find these plants a serious nuisance as they encroach on grazing land from established infestations on the perimeter of the land.

They are difficult to remove manually on account of their strong tap roots and can not efficiently absorb foliar-applied herbicides on account of their fine feathery leaves. A herbicide has been registered for wild asparagus. It does not cover all the various species, however, and great care must be taken with application and follow-up treatments.

Nothoscordum gracile

Protasparagus laricinus

COMMELINACEAE

Commelina africana
Yellow Wandering Jew, Eendagsblom

Commelina benghalensis
Wandering Jew, Benghal wandering Jew, Commelina, Wandelende Jood

Height: 0,4 – 2 m

Wandering Jew is one of the most serious and widespread annual weeds of South Africa. It is probably indigenous and although common throughout South Africa, it is most common in the summer rainfall regions.

C. benghalensis has small blue flowers which only last one or two hours. There are some closely related species with different coloured yellow flowers such as *C. africana*, which is an arable weed in tropical Africa. They are rarely a problem in South Africa, however.

C. benghalensis is a major weed of many crops. It competes strongly for moisture and in maize, it is a major late season weed. In other crops such as tea, it can climb into the bush interfering with growth and harvesting. Because of its creeping growth habit, one single plant can become very large and competitive.

Because of its vigorous growth and climbing habit, Wandering Jew is often grown as an indoor pot plant. In times of famine, the leaves are eaten by blacks.

Despite the fact that most of the vegetative growth and aerial seeds are produced above the ground, the plant also has burrowing runners. These runners are capable of producing underground flowers and seeds which are considerably larger than those produced above the ground. This is the main reason *C. benghalensis* is so difficult to control, as plants that grow from underground seeds cannot be killed by surface–applied herbicides until they emerge. This weed can also reproduce vegetatively, regenerating from small pieces that are broken from the parent plant.

Control is best achieved with post–emergence herbicides and deep cultivation. If control is attempted by means of cultivation, the cut stems must be buried deeper than 50 mm to kill them. Shallow cultivation only tends to spread the weed.

Commelina benghalensis

IRIDACEAE

Homeria miniata
Red tulp, Kraaitulp

Homeria pallida (=H. glauca)
Transvaal yellow tulp, Natal yellow tulp, Transvaalse geeltulp, Natalse geeltulp

Moraea polystachya
Blue tulp, Bloutulp

Height: 50 cm

There are approximately 70 indigenous species of 'tulp' in South Africa in the families *Homeria* and *Moraea*, most of them being poisonous.

They are perennial plants with a bulb or corm and leaves that are long and waxy, like tulip leaves. Flowering occurs from September to October and the plants are usually found in veld or pastures.

Different species occur in different areas with the examples above covering most of the country. The red tulp occurs in the south west regions and the blue tulp in the southern parts. The yellow tulp (which was originally thought to be two separate species), is found throughout the Transvaal and Natal.

Poisoning usually occurs during trekking of animals that come from a tulp free area. Animals raised in an infested area tend to avoid the plants unless grazing becomes scarce. They easily forget though, that tulp is poisonous, when moved to farms in areas where it occurs.

Sometimes farmers dose their cattle with a sauce made from fried bulbs, or wipe the mouths and nostrils of the cattle with an infusion of the bulbs and leaves. When released into an infested pasture, the cattle will then avoid eating tulp.

Chemical control of these weeds is very difficult and may only be achieved by wiping the leaves with a high concentration of a herbicide like glyphosate. It may help to scratch the leaves with a pot scourer first. Otherwise, successful control can only be achieved by physically digging up the bulbs, and ensuring that even the smallest bulblet is removed.

PINACEAE

Pinus patula
Patula pine, Patula-den, Treurden

Pinus pinaster
Cluster pine, Sparden

Height: 8 m

All *Pinus* species were introduced at one time or another, for commercial use.

P. pinaster was amongst the first to be planted for afforestation, having been estab-

Homeria pallida

Pinus pinaster

lished by the French Huguenots in 1825. Compared to the other species it has no value as timber. Some of the established plantations have spread and become unwanted weeds. The main infestations are still around Franschhoek in the Cape where the Huguenots first settled.

The cluster pine can be distinguished from other species by its paired, stout needles, the size and shape of its cone and the hook and ridge on the cone-scale tips.

P. patula and several other species of *Pinus* are planted commercially today and have become naturalised in the wild.

The seeds of pine trees, which are dispersed by wind, squirrels, baboons and other animals, germinate easily and establish themselves in cool, moist soil.

Large plants can be ring-barked, felled or treated with a soil-acting herbicide. Seedlings and saplings can be uprooted when the soil is moist or treated with a herbicide.

TYPHACEAE

Typha capensis
Bulrush, Papkuil, Palmiet

Height: 3 m

This is an indigenous species which is common throughout southern Africa. It is found in mud and slow flowing water which can be fresh or brackish and up to 1 m deep.

Bulrushes can be a problem by blocking water channels and interfering with the recreational use of the water. It also provides breeding sites for mosquitoes and harbours bilharzia-carrying snails. On the other hand, it harbours birds and wild life, traps silt and protects river banks against erosion.

Several herbicides have been registered for the control of bulrushes when necessary. They are all applied during the period of active growth prior to flowering but in each instance the product label should be read carefully to ascertain what precautions should be taken.

Typha capensis

DICOTYLEDONAE

AIZOACEAE

Aizoon glinoides
Aizoon

Height: 10 cm

This indigenous weed occurs in Zululand, the warm dry areas of the Natal Midlands such as Weenen, and is widespread in the Eastern Cape, especially on sandy soil.

It is a succulent weed and a relative of the 'vygie'. It is locally common, being a weed of annual crops such as planted sugar cane on the sandy soils of Zululand. *A. glinoides* is frequently found in many other areas of disturbed soil.

No herbicides have been registered for the control of this weed, but it is not usually a serious problem.

AIZOACEAE

Tetragonia caesia
Klappiesbrak

Height: 30 cm

A succulent, sprawling weed that is common in orchards and vineyards in the Cape. It is one of nearly forty indigenous species of *Tetragonia*, many of which are called 'klappiesbrak'.

Klappiesbrak is a problem in orchards for example, because it competes with precious water and nutrients. In many instances, however, it can be a life-saving fodder plant especially in dry areas.

No herbicide registrations exist, but klappiesbrak should be susceptible to the normal chemicals when small. It is easy to remove by cultivation.

AIZOACEAE

Zaleya pentandra
African purslane, Muisvygie

Height: 10 cm

A perennial, evergreen plant of uncertain origin but probably an exotic. African purslane is now a widespread weed in the sub-tropical parts of South Africa. It has been recorded in all provinces except the Orange Free State.

Aizoon glinoides

Tetragonia caesia

Zaleya pentandra

93

African purslane is commonly found in waste areas, old lands and disturbed soil, especially sandy soil.

It rarely becomes dense and competitive and there are no herbicides registered for its control. Cultivation will destroy it quite easily.

AMARANTHACEAE

Achyranthes aspera (=*A. argentea*)
Burweed, Chaff flower, Grootklits, Haak-en-steek-bossie

Height: 1 m

Of uncertain origin, but now pantropical in distribution, this perennial weed is found throughout the summer rainfall regions. Burweed occurs mainly in shady conditions such as in hedges, along streams, at the edge of patches of bush and in overgrown areas of gardens.

Before the production of the white flowers, this plant is rather plain and insignificant. As the flowers mature, the seeds turn downwards until they are lying along the stem, pointing to the ground. Being armed with sharp and unpleasant barbs, these seeds can penetrate the skin if the stalk is held carelessly.

Burweed is easily controlled by cultivation.

AMARANTHACEAE

Alternanthera pungens (=*A. repens*)
Khakiweed, Paperthorn, Khaki burweed, Kakiedubbeltjie

Height: 10 cm

A native of South America which, since the beginning of the 20th century, has spread to most areas of southern Africa. It is now of agronomic importance in the Transvaal Lowveld and the northern Transvaal.

It is said that burweed was introduced as an impurity of fodder brought in for the British troops (Khakies) during the Anglo-Boer War. The species followed the railway system and was usually first seen in areas near the stations, being easily spread on grain sacks as they were loaded and unloaded. It is a very unpleasant weed as the seeds can penetrate bare feet and even stick to rubber soled shoes. It also occurs in such places as lawns, gardens, pathways etc., and may not be noticed until trodden or sat upon, hence the names referring to 'thorn' or 'dubbeltjie'. (The old name 'repens' refers to its low, creeping growth habit). It has a large tap root and roots at the nodes, thereby forming large mats which are difficult to remove.

The common name 'khakiweed' is also commonly used for *Tagetes minuta*.

This weed is controlled effectively by many pre-emergence herbicides but becomes tolerant to post-emergence herbicides as it matures.

Achyranthes aspera

Alternanthera pungens

AMARANTHACEAE

Amaranthus deflexus
Perennial pigweed, Meerjarige misbredie

Amaranthus hybridus
Common pigweed, Cape pigweed, Redshank, Gewone misbredie, Kaapse misbredie

Amaranthus spinosus
Thorny pigweed, Doringmisbredie

Amaranthus thunberghii
Red pigweed, Rooimisbredie

Amaranthus viridis
Slender amaranth, Skraal misbredie

Height: 10 cm – 2 m

There are approximately 150 species of *Amaranthus* in South Africa of which nine are weeds. These five species are the most common. Only *A. thunberghii* is indigenous. They all tend to turn red as they mature.

A. deflexus is perennial, relatively short and sprawling, with a stout, fleshy taproot.

A. hybridus is said to be the most abundant and widely distributed broadleaf weed in southern Africa. It is also usually much taller than the other species.

A. spinosus has a pair of spines at the base of the leaves and is more troublesome in subtropical areas. Although it is well-known in cotton and tobacco, it is not so common in maize.

A. thunberghii has a much flatter growth habit than its relatives and tends to be more common on roadsides and in gardens than crops.

A. viridis is similar to *A. deflexus* but its central stem grows vertically and there are no flowers in the axils. They are frequently confused with each other.

These weedy species of *Amaranthus* are closely related to the ornamental varieties as well as those grown as grain crops in parts of Africa. These weeds are much favoured as a spinach by blacks and can even be found for sale on municipal markets. All species of *Amaranthus*, but *A. spinosus* in particular, are often found growing in rich, disturbed soils such as around kraals or cattle pens. Such plants contain high levels of nitrates which in ruminants, are converted to highly toxic nitrites by the micro-organisms present in the rumen. If eaten in excessive quantities by livestock this weed can cause severe poisoning and even death.

With the notable exception of bendioxide, all species of *Amaranthus* are susceptible to the normal broadleaf herbicides.

Amaranthus hybridus

Amaranthus thunberghii

Amaranthus viridis

Amaranthus deflexus

Amaranthus spinosus

AMARANTHACEAE

Cyathula uncinulata
Globe cyathula, Rondeklits

Height: 1,5 m

An indigenous species that is found throughout the temperate regions of South Africa.

A perennial weed with a deep tap root usually found in shaded places such as hedges and overgrown banks. The inflorescence is a round ball of hooked bristles which breaks away easily, contaminating the hair and wool of animals with consequent downgrading.

No herbicides have been registered specifically for this weed. It is best removed physically by cutting it below ground level.

AMARANTHACEAE

Gomphrena celosioides
Prostrate globe amaranth, Bachelor's button, Kruip–knopamarant, Mierbossie

Height: 20 cm

Prostrate globe amaranth is a native of tropical South America. It is now a cosmopolitan weed and widely distributed in the summer rainfall region of South Africa. It is commonly found in waste places and on roadsides but also in crops and gardens, particularly in neglected lawns.

This plant is quite different from the cultivated bachelor's button (*G. globosa*), which has purple flowers.

It is a weak competitor rarely requiring chemical control, but being a perennial, may need a systemic herbicide once it is well established. Seedlings are easy to remove by cultivation.

AMARANTHACEAE

Guilleminea densa (=Brayulinea densa)
Carrot weed

Height: 4 cm

Introduced from Central America, this plant is now a very troublesome weed in South Africa, mainly in the Transvaal. It was first recorded in Transvaal in 1909.

It is an annual plant, reproducing only from seed. The large, fleshy underground parts, however, can survive from year to year and for this reason it is a difficult weed to control.

Cyathula uncinulata

Guilleminea densa

Gomphrena celosioides

G. densa is a weed which causes serious problems on sports turf and golf courses, but is also found on roadsides, disturbed veld and on other sites.

Chemical control in grass swards will require repeated applications of selective herbicides. Removal by hand is difficult, because the plant can regrow from roots left behind. When using herbicides, it is always better to fertilize and avoid mowing for as long as possible prior to application. This allows the weed to become large, lush, vigorous and more capable of absorbing and translocating the herbicide.

APIACEAE

Ammi majus
Lace flower, Queen Anne's Lace, Kantblom

Height: 1 m

Introduced from Eurasia, this weed was and still is planted as an ornamental and for use in flower arrangements.

Lace flower has established itself in the wild and although found throughout South Africa, it is most common in the Cape where it is a nuisance in vineyards and orchards.

No herbicides have been registered for its control but the plants should be removed whilst still small as they become more resilient as they mature.

APIACEAE

Ciclospermum leptophyllum
Wild celery, Wildeseldery

Height: 45 cm

A native of Central America, wild celery is now widely distributed throughout the world.

Wild celery is widespread in South Africa and is usually found in damp places in gardens, cultivated lands and on river banks. In the eastern Lowveld in particular, wild celery can become dense and competitive and is occasionally a serious weed in sugar cane.

Chemical control is not effective on mature plants as once the above–ground foliage has been destroyed, it will readily regrow from parts remaining in the soil. Systemic herbicides should therefore be used where this weed is a problem.

It is easily controlled by shallow cultivation in the seedling stage.

Ammi majus

Ciclospermum leptophyllum

APIACEAE

Foeniculum vulgare
Wild fennel, Vinkel

Height: 2 m

Introduced from Europe as a horticultural crop during the early settler days, fennel has escaped into the wild and is now found throughout South Africa. It is especially common in the Cape where it has become invasive.

When crushed it has a very strong, characteristic smell and is therefore a nuisance in wheat, especially in the Swartland. When infested fields are harvested, the fennel can be smelt from a considerable distance. The grain from these fields, being contaminated with the smell of fennel, are rejected at the silo.

Wild fennel is a perennial plant, reproducing only by seed. Perennial individuals are only usually found in such places as roadsides and waste places. In wheat they must seed down each season.

No herbicides have been registered for this weed and it is best removed by physical methods.

APIACEAE

Hydrocotyle americana
Navelwort, Water pennywort, Perdekloutjies

Height: 15 cm

Navelwort is a cosmopolitan weed of uncertain origin. It is probably exotic.

It is a perennial, evergreen plant with shiny leaves that are often yellow–green in colour. It is widely distributed in the summer rainfall areas and commonly found in damp places in gardens, lawns, golf greens and in any moist and sheltered spot. It can grow up to about 15 cm tall, but will flourish even under heavy mowing, such as on golf greens, although the leaves often become much smaller. It flowers when allowed to grow lank, and will produce seeds. Once established, spreading is accomplished by running stems that root at the internodes and by rhizomes.

Because of its perennial nature, control is difficult. Repeated applications of selective herbicides may be necessary in grass swards such as golf greens.

Foeniculum vulgare

Hydrocotyle americana

103

ASCLEPIADACEAE

Araujia sericifera
Moth catcher, Bladder flower, Motvanger

Height: 3 – 5 m

A native of Peru that was introduced into South Africa as an ornamental. It is now found in many parts of South Africa as a weed of gardens, waste areas and plantations.

It is a robust, semi–woody, perennial creeper that can reach the top of tall trees. It exudes a white juice and the fruit is a large spongy capsule.

There are no recommended control methods, but this plant should be uprooted when small.

ASCLEPIADACEAE

Asclepias fruticosa
Shrubby milkweed, Firesticks, Melkbos, Wildekapok, Tontelbos

Asclepias physocarpa
Milkweed, Balbos

Height: 1 – 2 m

These are widespread indigenous weeds, commonly found on roadsides, in unused lands, vleis, along watercourses and in the veld.

A. fruticosa is more common in the Transvaal and O.F.S. and has a shrubby growth habit and a pointed fruit. *A. physocarpa* is prevalent in Natal and has a rounded fruit. Both species have been accidentally introduced into South Africa from Australia.

The fruit is a balloon-like structure with long processes like hairs. The seeds are numerous, turning from brown to black as they ripen and each has a plume of long silky hairs. These plumes have been used as a substitute for kapok and in the past were used in the making of tinder in tinder boxes, hence the Afrikaans name 'tontelbos'.

If eaten by livestock, which is rare as these weeds are unpalatable, they are toxic. The plants contain heart glycosoids which cause the same symptoms as tulp poisoning.

Milkweed should be controlled by physical means when still young.

Araujia sericifera

Asclepias fruticosa

Asclepias physocarpa

105

ASTERACEAE

Acanthospermum australe
Prostrate starbur, Eight-seeded starbur, Kruipsterklits, Donkieklits

Acanthospermum brasilum
Brazilian starbur, Five-seeded starbur, Brasiliaanse sterklits

Acanthospermum hispidum
Upright starbur, Regopsterklits

Height: 10 - 60 cm

These 'starburs', which are of South American origin and were probably introduced in imported fodder during the Anglo-Boer War, are now common weeds of crops in the warmer parts of South Africa. They are of particular importance in the northern and eastern Transvaal.

The burs on these weeds contaminate sheep's wool and cause subsequent downgrading.

A. australe and *A. brasilium* are considered by some authorities to be the same species. Certainly, the only major difference is the number of seeds in the inflorescence, (5 and 8-9 respectively).

A. hispidum is a closely related, annual species with a more upright growth habit, and can be more of a problem because of this as it is more likely to contaminate a crop. *A. hispidum* can for instance, contaminate cotton lint and cause the downgrading thereof.

Shallow cultivation and most broadleaf herbicides are successful in controlling these weeds.

ASTERACEAE

Achillea millefolium
Common yarrow, Milfoil, Duisendblaar-achillea

Height: 1 m

A perennial plant that was introduced from Europe as an ornamental. It has now become naturalised in many parts of the country.

It is commonly found on roadsides and in waste places. Common yarrow is not usually a problem in cultivated lands except when it occurs in perennial pastures. It has been reported as a contaminant of various kinds of commercial seed, especially grass seed.

No specific herbicide has been registered for this weed, but as it is a perennial, it will probably require the use of a systemic chemical to eradicate it successfully.

Acanthospermum hispidum

Acanthospermum australe

Achillea millefolium

ASTERACEAE

Ageratum conyzoides
Invading ageratum, Blue weed, Billy-goat weed, Indringer-ageratum, Bokkruid

Ageratum houstonianum
Garden ageratum, Todd's curse, Tuinageratum

Height: 1 m

These are common tropical and sub-tropical weeds of South American origin.

They are plants that are often cultivated in gardens but have become very widespread weeds. *A. conyzoides* is common in most of the warmer areas of the eastern part of the country, whereas *A. houstonianum* is dominant in the Natal Midlands. It is called Todd's curse after a nurseryman who lived in Pietermaritzburg during the nineteenth century and was first recorded as a weed in 1883. It is distinguished by its relatively large flower heads.

Ageratum is a common weed of annual crops and can invade perennial crops such as sugar cane. It is also known as a weed of roadsides, riverbanks and other crops. On occasion it can be a serious problem in cotton. The wind–blown seeds contaminate the lint and irritate the pickers' eyes.

In various parts of the world, *A. conyzoides* is used in medicines and folk remedies. The leaves are often used as a wound dressing and in the West Indies, for example, a tea is made that is used to treat a variety of ailments.

It is relatively easy to control by cultivation and pre-emergence herbicides. However, once it has matured it is difficult to control with many of the post-emergence chemicals.

ASTERACEAE

Anthemis arvensis
Corn chamomile, Wild chamomile, Wildekamille

Anthemis cotula
Dogfennel, Stinking mayweed, Stinkkamille

Height: 75 cm

These are two species of chamomile from Europe and Asia which are now established weeds in South Africa.

A. cotula in particular, was probably introduced as an ornamental, but both are now weeds of pastures and cereals. The seeds are easily dispersed as a contaminant of the pasture seeds.

No specific herbicides have been registered for the control of these weeds.

Ageratum conyzoides

Anthemis cotula

109

ASTERACEAE

Arctotis venusta
Free State daisy, Witgousblom

Height: 30 cm

An indigenous species that has become a troublesome weed in the O.F.S. and parts of the Karoo.

Although unpalatable, it is thought to be mildly poisonous and can taint milk. It is planted in gardens as an ornamental.

When it occurs in crops it responds to conventional herbicides and can be removed by cultivation.

ASTERACEAE

Arctotheca calendula (=*Cryptostemma calendulaceum*)
Cape marigold, Cape weed, Gousblom

Height: 75 cm

As the name suggests, this indigenous weed is widespread in the Cape Province, and is especially prevalent along the south–western coast and in vineyards. It is a well known weed in most of the wheat areas of the Cape. It has also been recorded in a few areas of Natal and the O.F.S.

It is thought to taint the milk of animals that eat it.

Cape marigold is easily controlled in wheat by most post–emergence herbicides, especially MCPA. Diquat is usually better than paraquat in minimum tillage situations.

ASTERACEAE

Berkheya erysithales

Berkheya macrocephala

Berkheya rigida
Disseldoring

Height: 0,5 – 1,5 m

There are many indigenous species of *Berkheya*. Some, like these are thistle–like and can, because of their unpleasant spines, become a nuisance in grazing and on roadsides.

B. macrocephala and *B. erysithales* can be found in Natal and the Cape, whereas *B. rigida* is widespread but especially common and troublesome in parts of the Cape.

There are no herbicides registered for these weeds and they are best controlled by physical means.

Arctotis venusta

Arctotheca calendula

Berkheya erysithales

Berkheya macrocephala

Berkheya rigida

111

ASTERACEAE

Bidens bipinnata
Spanish blackjack, Spaanse knapsekêrel

Bidens pilosa
Common blackjack,Gewone knapsekêrel

Height: 1 m

Both these weeds were introduced during the last century, *B. bipinnata* from Eurasia, and *B. pilosa* from South America. They are now common, widespread and extremely troublesome, being found in most crops and disturbed areas.

These two closely related weeds which often hybridise, are well–known to South Africans. Their fruit are the unpleasant 'blackjacks' that stick to clothing, hair etc., being able to burrow rapidly through several layers of clothing. Each little blackjack has tiny barbs and rough edges allowing it to burrow like this. This is an extremely efficient method of dispersal.

A third species of blackjack (*B. biternata*), is occasionally found. It is similar to *B. pilosa* with its broader leaves, but the leaves are usually divided into five leaflets, with the lowermost pair re-divided into two to three segments.

The leaves are eaten by blacks as a spinach.

Blackjacks often germinate in dense mats. This uniform, shallow germination fortunately means that they are relatively easy to control, especially with post-emergence herbicides.

ASTERACEAE

Bidens formosa (=*Cosmos bipinnatus*)
Cosmos, Kosmos, Mieliepes

Height: 1,5 m

A native of Central America and the West Indies, cosmos is now widespread in South Africa. It was introduced in fodder during the Anglo-Boer War and was originally recorded as being naturalised in Pretoria in 1904. This weed did not spread to Natal until 1945.

Cosmos is not always an unwanted weed as the dazzling autumnal displays of this flower along roadsides are spectacular. However, they spread into nearby fields and become a nuisance. These displays are most memorable in the higher-lying areas of Natal, the O.F.S. and the Transvaal Highveld.

The flowers are white, pink and occasionally, dark purple; the ratio varying from place to place. Sometimes the flowers in a certain area are nearly all white and sometimes, predominantly pink. Very occasionally, banks of the dark purple variety can be seen.

Bidens bipinnata

Bidens pilosa

Bidens formosa

113

This is a genetic characteristic and is not the result of any influence exerted by the nature of the soil or climate.

Several varieties with larger flowers have been bred for the garden and can flower at other times of the year.

Cosmos is susceptible to cultivation and many broadleaf weed herbicides.

ASTERACEAE

Blumea gariepina
Wolbos

Height: 1,25 m

An indigenous perennial shrub that is widespread in South Africa but common mainly in the northern Transvaal.

It is a weed of veld, grazing, fallow lands and orchards, occasionally become dense and dominating, thereby eliminating any grass that may have been present.

B. gariepina must not be confused with the *Conyza* spp.

It is thought to taint the milk of animals that eat it.

There are no herbicides registered for this weed, but unless the plants are destroyed as seedlings, the mature plants can only be pulled out by hand.

ASTERACEAE

Cenia turbinata (=*Cotula turbinata*)
Goose daisy, Mayweed, Ganskos

Height: 40 cm

Goose daisy is found mainly in the Cape Province in the winter rainfall areas. It is an indigenous weed of gardens, orchards, waste places, roadsides and agricultural crops occasionally becoming a problem in cereals. It has a distinctive smell and the flowers can be yellow or white.

Goose daisy is usually only of nuisance value and it can easily be removed by cultivation. It is susceptible to the usual broadleaf weed herbicides.

Blumea gariepina

Cenia turbinata

ASTERACEAE

Centaurea cyanus
Cornflower, Koringblom

Centaurea melitensis
Malta centaurea, Malta–centaurea, Maltadissel

Centaurea repens
Russian centaurea, Russiese centaurea, Russiese dissel

Centaurea solstitialis
Yellow centaurea, Geelcentaurea

Height: 1 m

These four species of *Centaurea* from Eurasia were introduced as ornamentals or as seed impurities up to a hundred years ago, and are now weeds in South Africa.

The blue *C. cyanus* occurs in wheat fields of the Cape. The yellow *C. melitensis* from Malta is better known in lucerne fields and along roadsides, both having been spread as impurities in cultivated seed. *C. melitensis* was first collected from the Cape Flats in 1865 but was probably introduced into Natal and Transvaal 10 years previously with contaminated oat seed. *C. solstitialis* first appeared in the 1920s.

The other two are somewhat restricted in distribution, tending to be found only in parts of the Cape Province. *C. solstitialis* is also yellow but with longer 'spines' than *C. melitensis*. *C. repens* is purple or pink.

No herbicides have been registered for the control of these weeds but when small, they should succumb to normal broadleaf–weed herbicides and shallow cultivation.

ASTERACEAE

Chromolaena odorata (=Eupatorium odoratum)
Paraffin weed, Triffid weed, Paraffienbos

Height: 3 – 8 m

A native of South America which was first recorded in the south-western Cape in 1858 where it did not survive. It was probably reintroduced into Natal in about 1947.

Paraffin weed is now a major perennial weed in the coastal region of Natal and the Eastern Transvaal Lowveld. It is a serious problem in many other countries such as the Philippines, Nigeria, Sri Lanka, Australia and the Ivory Coast. It is not classified as a weed in South America where it originated, probably because it has a range of natural enemies there. The leaves have a characteristic smell when crushed.

It is thought to have been mistakenly introduced into Natal in packing materials contaminated with the seed that was off-loaded at Durban harbour during the Second World War. It soon established itself as a weed, and by 1962 was reported as spreading

Centaurea cyanus

Centaurea melitensis

Chromolaena odorata

117

'virulently' along the coastal areas. It invaded even undisturbed vegetation, totally swamping and replacing the indigenous species. Triffid weed is now found in almost any situation, clogging areas such as stream banks, indigenous bush and gardens. In forestry plantations it invades clear–felled areas with its wind-blown seeds. Because it is highly inflammable, even when green, it allows grass fires to penetrate deep into forestry compartments.

It is said to be poisonous to horses.

Control of this weed is difficult and costly because it is capable of vigorous regrowth from stem coppice, root suckers and seed. Large plants must be cut down and the tops removed and burned, whereafter a suitable herbicide should be applied to the stump or regrowth. Small plants can be pulled out by hand when the soil is moist, and care should be taken to remove as much root material as possible. Care should also be taken with follow-up inspections and treatment to ensure that all traces have been eliminated.

A beetle is raising hopes of biological control following successes overseas. However, so far it has failed to establish itself where it was released into Natal, but work is progressing along these lines.

ASTERACEAE

Chrysanthemum segetum
Corn chrysanthemum, Koringkrisant

Height: 50 cm

This annual weed, which is a native of western Asia and southern Europe, is now cosmopolitan. In South Africa it was first recorded in 1904 in the Belfast district in Transvaal, where it was possibly cultivated as an ornamental and then escaped. It has spread to the Eastern Cape where it is now found in wheat and vegetables. It is no longer found in the Transvaal.

It is not often a serious weed and although not covered by a herbicide registration it should be susceptible to the usual broadleaf weed herbicides used in wheat. Chemical control in vegetables is more difficult. Where a problem exists, a rotation with a cereal will offer the best prospects of long term control.

ASTERACEAE

Cichorium intybus
Chicory, Sigorei

Height: 1,5 m

Originally from Eurasia, chicory was introduced into South Africa for cultivation. It has escaped into the wild and is now a widespread perennial weed, occurring in most situations, especially fallow land and roadsides.

Chrysanthemum segetum

Cichorium intybus

The roasted roots are used as a supplement or substitute for coffee and the blanched young shoots are edible. The plant exudes a milky juice when broken and has stout tap roots and large basal leaves.

Chicory is not often a serious weed in cultivated lands and no specific herbicides have been registered. It should be susceptible to the usual herbicides as long as the plant is not allowed to get too big.

ASTERACEAE

Cirsium arvense
Creeping thistle, Canada thistle, Kanadese dissel

Cirsium vulgare
Spear thistle, Scotch thistle, Speerdissel, Skotse dissel

Height: 1,5 m

These two species of thistle are natives of Europe and Asia which have spread to virtually all temperate zones of the world.

C. vulgare is now a proclaimed weed in South Africa where it is widespread and common, except in lowveld areas. It was first recorded from Van Reenen in Natal and it is thought to have been introduced with imported hay or fodder during the Boer War.

It is usually a weed of pastures, waste places and along roadsides, preferring moist, rich soil. It does not thrive on regularly cultivated lands.

The species is biennial. During the first year it germinates in autumn and a deep tap root is developed. The second year the flowering stem will shoot up, often to over 1 m in height, producing the typical spiny flowers. The plant flowers late in spring or early in summer and produces an abundance of seeds, each with a silky plume. This plume helps the dispersal of the seed by acting as a kind of parachute. Birds eat the seed and also collect the silky plumes for their nests. The seeds are also spread around the farm in bales of contaminated stock feed.

Spear thistle is easily controlled with regular cultivation and is susceptible to hormone herbicides as well as to many of the contact type. Good veld management however, is of utmost importance in the long term control of this weed. In fact, spear thistle infestations in veld is a barometer for poor veld management.

C. arvense, although a symbol of Canada, is also from Eurasia. It is believed to have been introduced into Canada as an impurity of seed which is probably the same route it took to South Africa. It is not as common or as widespread in South Africa as C. vulgare as it has not been recorded from Natal or the O.F.S.

Canada thistle is dioecious, which means that the sexes are separate plants. If a plant of the opposite sex is not nearby no fertile seeds will be produced. It can reproduce by means of seeds (if possible), or from underground rhizomes. The latter method is asexual so does not require the presence of different sexes, rather it is just an extension of

Cirsium vulgare

the original plant. A system of such underground rhizomes can extend over quite a large area.

An unpleasant problem in pastures, gardens and in wasteland, this thistle is fortunately very susceptible to the non-selective, systemic herbicides. Infestations in crops and pastures should be isolated and spot-sprayed. If being removed by hand, care must be taken to remove all the pieces of rhizome which are capable of regrowing if left.

ASTERACEAE

Conyza albida (=*Erigeron floribundis*/*Conyza sumatrensis*)
Tall fleabane, Vaalskraalhans

Conyza bonariensis (=*Erigeron bonariensis*)
Flax–leaf fleabane, Horseweed, Kleinskraalhans, Armoedskruid

Conyza canadensis (=*Erigeron canadensis*)
Horseweed fleabane, Kanadese skraalhans

Conyza podocephala
Conyza, Oondbos

Height: 1 – 2 m

Of the 15 species of *Conyza* that occur in South Africa, four were introduced from the Americas; three of them are here, and these three are the major weeds. They are closely related species, similar in habit and distribution, which is widespread.

C. bonariensis grows to about 1,2 m and has lateral branches taller than the main stem. *C. canadensis* is also relatively short but has smaller flowers and is unbranched. *C. albida* grows to over 2 m and never has side stems taller than the main axis. They can often be found growing together.

C. podocephala is an indigenous species with a strong tap root and sometimes produces runners.

These are common annual weeds of gardens, roadsides, fallow land and forestry and to a lesser extent, annual crops. Perennial crops often become infested. Fleabane can become a serious problem in sugar cane, particularly ratoon cane or cane which has been neglected for a while. Fleabane is an important weed in crops under minimum tillage and must not be allowed to become too tall before treating it with herbicides. They are also becoming well-known as winter weeds of maize lands.

Fleabane is susceptible to pre-emergence herbicides but shallow cultivation and the application of post-emergence herbicides must be completed before plants form a rosette, otherwise it will not be effective.

Conyza albida

Conyza bonariensis

Conyza canadensis

Conyza podocephala

ASTERACEAE

Coreopsis lanceolata
Tickseed

Height: 60 cm

A native of the eastern United States that was introduced as an ornamental. It has now become naturalised in South Africa and is commonly found on roadsides and railway embankments in the summer rainfall areas.

In Natal it was first recorded as having escaped from cultivation on the roadside at Kloof in 1955. It is thus a relatively recent introduction. It can on occasion, be observed near neglected graveyards where seed has escaped from cut plants put on graves.

It is a perennial with underground rhizomes, and once it becomes established, it is difficult to eradicate. Systemic herbicides should therefore be used for effective eradication.

ASTERACEAE

Cotula australis
Cotula

Height: 20 cm

Originating in Australia, *C. australis* now occurs throughout most of the Southern hemisphere. In South Africa, it was originally observed at Grahamstown in 1868; since then it has gradually spread northwards, possibly as far as Swaziland.

It is usually a weed of damp and shady places but also appears able to withstand direct sunlight. It is therefore found in lawns and golf greens where it can be a problem.

C. australis flowers throughout the year and for this reason, it is noticed more in winter than at other times of the year.

There are many other species of *Cotula*, some of which have escaped from cultivation and some that are indigenous.

No herbicides have been registered to control *Cotula*, but in most situations it can easily be removed by cultivation. In lawns and golf greens, however, it appears fairly hardy and repeated applications of selective broadleaf herbicides may be necessary.

ASTERACEAE

Eclipta prostrata (=E. alba)
Eclipta

Height: 1 m

Eclipta originates from Europe and Asia and is now cosmopolitan in the warmer parts of the world. It has been known in South Africa for over 70 years and is an annual

Coreopsis lanceolata

Cotula australis

Cotula sp.

Eclipta prostrata

125

weed of many situations, but preferring damp places. It is distributed mainly in the summer rainfall region, but is found throughout the country with the exception of the O.F.S.

There are no registered control measures but eclipta is unlikely to become economically significant. Cultivation and conventional herbicides should give adequate control.

ASTERACEAE

Flaveria bidentis
Smelter's bush, Smelterbossie

Height: 1 m

A native of tropical America, probably having been introduced in imported fodder during the Anglo-Boer War, that has spread rapidly in South Africa. Smelter's bush is most common in the northern and eastern Transvaal, northern Cape and Namibia but found throughout the country with the exception of the southern and eastern Cape.

It is a common annual weed of crops, gardens and waste places, occasionally becoming dense and competitive.

Smelter's bush is very easy to control with shallow cultivation and conventional herbicides.

ASTERACEAE

Galinsoga ciliata
Hairy galinsoga

Galinsoga parviflora
Small-flowered quickweed, Gallant soldier, Knopkruid

Height: 60 cm

G. parviflora, originally from South America but now a cosmopolitan annual weed, is troublesome in a wide range of crops throughout South Africa except the south-western Cape. When dense it can become very competitive.

G. ciliata, also from South America, can easily be confused with G. parviflora, but is more hairy and only occurs in Natal and the eastern Transvaal. Both species can often be found growing together.

These weeds are on record as alternate hosts for some nematode species as well as for the tobacco and cucumber mosaic virus.

Galinsoga is easy to control in most situations as it is a shallow germinator. In wheat, however, it is relatively tolerant to some of the non-hormonal herbicides, therefore herbicide mixtures may have to be considered.

Flaveria bidentis

Galinsoga parviflora

ASTERACEAE

Gnaphalium pensylvanicum
Gnaphalium

Height: 60 cm

Originally from North America, G. pensylvanicum is now a widespread annual weed in the warmer parts of the world such as Australia, the Middle East and China. In South Africa, it was first recorded in Natal in 1865. It is now common in most of the eastern parts of the country, from the eastern Cape through the Transkei and Natal to Swaziland and the Lowveld.

It occurs as a weed of gardens, lands, orchards and other damp places up to an altitude of about 1 200 m. It is well-known as a weed in conservation-tillage maize.

Despite being a common and widespread weed, G. pensylvanicum does not appear to have a common name.

It can be controlled by shallow cultivation and is susceptible to conventional herbicides.

ASTERACEAE

Helichrysum cooperi
Geelsewejaartjie, Sewejaartjie

Helichrysum ruderale
Height: 1,5 m

Two very closely related species that are indigenous and occur on the entire eastern side of the country. There are also several other similar species with which they can be confused. They both have yellow, 'everlasting' flowers. The leaves have a very strong smell, are woolly and become sticky as they mature. H. cooperi flowers in the summer whereas H. ruderale flowers in the spring (Sept – Oct).

H. ruderale in particular, forms dense stands along roadsides and in old fields.

Chemical control should be initiated when the plants are small as they become more tolerant as soon as vertical growth commences.

Seedlings are easily removed by cultivation.

ASTERACEAE

Hypochoeris radicata
Hairy wild lettuce, Spotted cat's ear, Harige skaapslaai, Skaapslaai, Kat-oor

Height: 0,5 m

Introduced from Europe, this plant is now a cosmopolitan weed and is widespread in South Africa.

Gnaphalium pensylvanicum

Helichrysum ruderale

Hypochoeris radicata

H. radicata is mostly a weed of gardens, roadsides and waste places and is seldom a weed of annual crops, except in crops like maize when under conservation tillage. It might occasionally infest orchards, pastures and other perennial crops.

The leaves of young plants are eaten by blacks.

It has fleshy rhizomes and numerous fibrous roots making chemical control difficult once it has become established and will require systemic broadleaf herbicides.

ASTERACEAE

Inula graveolens
Cape khakiweed, Camphor inula, Kaapse kakiebos, Kanfer–inula

Height: 1 m

Originally from the Mediterranean region of Europe and having been introduced at the time of the Anglo-Boer War, this plant is now a major perennial weed in parts of the Cape Province. It is not found north of the Karoo.

Cape khakiweed is a major problem in wheat lands as it has a very strong and distinctive smell which can contaminate the grain. It will continue to grow after the field has been cut. It is also common in other crops, waste places and on roadsides. The plant is covered with glandular hairs that make it sticky to the touch.

It is unpalatable to cattle but if they do eat it, it can taint the milk and also cause oxalate poisoning.

Once it has become established, Cape khakiweed is very difficult to control on account of its strong root system. It should be controlled before it reaches the five–leaf stage, either physically or chemically.

ASTERACEAE

Lactuca serriola
Wild lettuce, Wildeslaai

Height: 2 m

A native of Europe and now a widespread weed in South Africa on roadsides and in crops and gardens.

Although wild lettuce can be perennial, it often behaves as an annual, especially in annual crops. It is therefore easy to control with shallow cultivation and is susceptible to pre- and post-emergence herbicides.

Inula graveolens

Lactuca serriola

ASTERACEAE

Mantisalca salmantica (=*Centaurea salmantica*)
Mantisalca

Height: 1 m

This plant was probably introduced from Eurasia with the centaureas over a century ago.

M. salmantica has a very limited distribution, being found almost exclusively in the vicinity of Aberdeen in the Cape. It is showing no signs of spreading. It is, however, very common in the area and it is a problem on the roadsides and in the fields and gardens of the area.

There are no recommendations for the control of this weed.

ASTERACEAE

Matricaria nigellifolia
Bovine staggers plant, Staggers weed, Rivierals, Stootsiektebossie, Waterkerwel

Height: 60 cm

An indigenous weed that occurs throughout South Africa. It prefers moist areas and is usually found in marshes, near dams and on river banks. It can even grow in water.

If consumed it can be fatal to cattle, causing what is commonly called 'bovine staggers', 'pushing disease', or 'stootsiekte'. The animal has protruding eyeballs and staggers around with its head held low which it pushes against solid objects such as trees or posts. This ultimately leads to death and severe losses are sometimes recorded. Despite the wide distribution of the weed, the poisoning appears to occur mainly in Natal, especially the Natal Midlands. The Mooi River valley is a prime example.

Chemical control is not very successful and where poisoning occurs, the infested areas should rather be fenced off.

ASTERACEAE

Nidorella resedifolia
Stinkkruid, Wurmbossie

Height: 1,5 m

An indigenous, annual plant that occurs as a weed in the sub-tropical areas of the summer rainfall region, but it has been recorded in all provinces. It can become a nuisance in citrus orchards for example and is especially common in the Pongola area of Natal.

Matricaria nigellifolia

Mantisalca salmantica

Nidorella resedifolia

No specific herbicides have been registered for this weed but it is easily controlled by cultivation.

ASTERACEAE

Osteospermum clandestinum
Daisy

Height: 50 cm

An indigenous and common annual weed around Cape Town and the western districts. It is found in waste places, roadsides, orchards and vineyards.

There are about 80 indigenous species of *Osteospermum* that are all generally called 'daisies' but only one or two are considered weeds. There are also the occasional exotic daisies that have escaped from gardens and can be found growing in fields and on roadsides.

Various species of daisy make up a large proportion of the spectacular floral displays in the Western Cape. However, this species in particular is more widespread and aggressive and becomes an undesirable plant in many situations.

Daisies are generally easy to control when necessary by cultivation.

ASTERACEAE

Parthenium hysterophorus
Parthenium, Demoina weed

Height: 1,5 m

Parthenium is an introduced, perennial weed from North America that has been known in Natal for many years after probably having been introduced during the Anglo-Boer War. It has spread extensively into Swaziland and is now causing a serious problem in some areas.

Occurring in crops, on roadsides and in waste places, it has also invaded the natural vegetation of game parks in Swaziland to a considerable degree, especially where the veld has been overgrazed. In the eastern Transvaal Lowveld, where they call this plant Demoina weed, it suddenly appeared after cyclone Demoina in 1983. It is quite possible that seeds were picked up by the strong cyclonic winds in Swaziland and transported to the Lowveld where it is now a major nuisance in sugar cane and bananas.

In Australia, it spread rapidly after introduction and is now considered to be one of their worst weeds. Meanwhile researchers are searching for biological control agents. In India, parthenium is blamed for a form of dermatitis.

In South Africa, it is not yet a widespread problem but it obviously has a high potential to become one. A closely related species, commonly called guayule, is being grown

Osteospermum clandestinum

Parthenium hysterophorus

135

experimentally in South Africa as an alternative source of natural rubber.

Parthenium seems to be tolerant to many chemicals. Systemic, non–selective chemicals should be used, and where feasible, individual plants should be pulled out by hand before they set seed.

ASTERACEAE

Picris echioides
Bristly oxtongue, Stekelrige beestong, Ostong, Stekel-picris

Height: 1,5 m

An annual weed which is a native of central and southern Europe the bristly oxtongue is now fairly widespread, especially in the Cape.

It is usually found in waste places and on roadsides, but can become a problem in orchards and vineyards. The leaves have small bristles, hence the name.

It is susceptible to non-selective herbicides such as paraquat, especially when young.

ASTERACEAE

Pseudognaphalium luteo-album (=*Gnaphalium luteo-album*)
Jersey cudweed, Roerkruid

Pseudognaphalium undulatum
Cudweed, Groenbossie

Height: 40 cm

Jersey cudweed is a widespread and common annual weed from Europe. It tends to invade old lands, waste places and roadsides. It was introduced by early settlers.

It is well-known as a winter weed of maize lands. It will grow densely the following summer if the field is not cultivated as in reduced-tillage systems. This weed has readily become a problem in wheat in parts of the O.F.S.

When mature, it is rather tolerant to herbicides but is susceptible to shallow cultivation as a seedling. It does not seem to respond well to the sulphonyl urea group of herbicides.

Cudweed, *P. undulatum*, is indigenous and widespread in South Africa. It is most likely to be found in waste places and on roadsides.

No herbicides have been registered for cudweed.

Picris echioides

Pseudognaphalium luteo-album

ASTERACEAE

Schkuhria pinnata
Dwarf marigold, Kleinkakiebos

Height: 40 cm

A common annual weed from South America, the dwarf marigold is now a pest of many crops, especially in the summer rainfall region. It occasionally becomes competitive.

It was first recorded in South Africa in 1898. The Afrikaans name derives from the fact that British soldiers ('khakies'), introduced this weed with imported fodder for their horses.

It is said that this plant will taint the milk of cattle that have eaten it.

Dwarf marigold is generally well controlled by the normal pre- and post-emergence herbicides.

ASTERACEAE

Senecio chrysocoma

Senecio consanguineus
Starvation senecio, Ragwort, Hongerbos-senecio, Bankrotbos, Radiatorbossie

Senecio latifolius
Ragwort, Krakerbossie

Senecio madagascariensis

Senecio polyanthemoides

Height: 1 – 1,5 m

These are some of the other species of 'ragwort' that are common weeds of crops, gardens, roadsides and waste places.

S. consanguineus is found in the northern Cape, O.F.S., Namibia, Botswana and the Transvaal highveld. It is an annual, germinating in late summer and remaining green during winter. During soil preparation the following season, the light, fluffy seeds tend to block the radiators of tractors, hence the common name 'radiator' weed, particularly in the western Transvaal.

S. latifolius is known to be toxic and occurs mainly in Natal. It is an annual that can survive more than one season.

S. madagascariensis is very common in the eastern parts of the country.

S. polyanthemoides occurs from Port St. Johns, through Natal to the mountains of the Eastern Transvaal, Swaziland and into Mozambique. It grows naturally on forest mar-

Schkuhria pinnata

Senecio latifolius

Senecio madagascariensis

Senecio consanguineus

Senecio polyanthemoides

gins, but is an abundant weed along roadsides, in old fields and in felled plantations. The pale under-surface of the leaves is a result of very small fine hairs.

S. chrysocoma is common on roadsides in Natal.

These weeds can be controlled by shallow cultivation when young.

ASTERACEAE

Senecio ilicifolius
Sprinkaan-senecio

Senecio inaequidens (=*S. burchellii*)
Molteno disease senecio, Canary weed, Burchell-senecio, Geelopslag

Height: 1 – 2 m

The *Senecio* genus is the largest of all the flowering plants, with over 2 000 known species worldwide and up to 350 occurring in South Africa.

Many species of *Senecio* contain toxic substances and some cause animal or even human poisoning, although the majority are not known to be toxic. These two indigenous species have been proclaimed noxious weeds because they were implicated in cases of 'bread poisoning' in the Riversdale region of the Cape. Parts of the plant contaminated harvested wheat and poisoning occurred when the bread made from this wheat was consumed. Fortunately, grazing animals find *Senecio* unpalatable and will usually only eat the plants by accident. However, if sufficient quantities are consumed, fatal poisoning can occur. In horses in particular, the poison can be accumulative.

S. inaequidens is a perennial weed found mainly in the Cape especially in the Ceres, Middelburg and Prieska areas.

S. ilicifolius is primarily an annual, restricted to areas between George and East London.

Apart from being common in wheat lands, these weeds are also found in other crops, gardens, on roadsides and in waste places.

These plants can be controlled by shallow cultivation when young, and are susceptible to many of the usual broadleaf weed herbicides.

ASTERACEAE

Sigesbeckia orientalis
St. Paul's wort, Pauluskruid

Height: 1 m

An annual weed of uncertain origin. It is probably exotic, being a widespread weed in the tropics of the Old World. In South Africa it occurs from the Soutpansberg to Port St. Johns. It has not been recorded in the O.F.S.

Senecio ilicifolius

Sigesbeckia orientalis

141

St. Paul's wort is commonly found on forest margins, in waste areas and gardens, only occasionally becoming a weed of economic importance and then only in high-rainfall areas.

It is not usually aggressive, but where control measures are necessary it is susceptible to chemicals and cultivation.

ASTERACEAE

Sonchus asper
Spiny sowthistle, Doringsydissel

Sonchus oleraceus
Sowthistle, Milkthistle, Sydissel, Tuindissel

Height: 1,5 m

The spiny sowthistle and sowthistle are two of the earliest weeds introduced into South Africa from Europe, *S. oleraceus* having been recorded at the Cape as early as 1685.

These two thistles are both annuals and very similar in appearance but the leaf margins of *S. asper* are spiny, especially when mature.

The sowthistles are widespread in cultivated fields and gardens. The leaves are eaten as a salad and the milky roots are said to be good for bread making.

These weeds are most effectively controlled by clean cultivation followed by hand-weeding of scattered plants. The plants should be destroyed before the seeds are set. They are well-controlled by pre- and post-emergence broadleaf herbicides.

ASTERACEAE

Spilanthes decumbens
Spilanthes

Height: 25 cm

A native of Uruguay that is adventive in South Africa. This means that it is a relatively recent introduction, but is now established and spreading. It was first recorded at East London in 1926 but has spread to most parts of the eastern half of the country. It often forms dense colonies, especially on roadsides.

It is not a serious weed at present. It is, however, a good example of an exotic species establishing itself and having the potential to spread into a variety of niches and displace indigenous vegetation.

It is controlled effectively by triazines, but only pre-emergent.

Sonchus asper

Spilanthes decumbens

Sonchus oleraceus

143

ASTERACEAE

Tagetes minuta
Tall khaki weed, Mexican marigold, Langkakiebos, Kakiebos

Height: 1 – 2 m

Originating in South America, this is a very common, widespread and serious annual weed in many crops, particularly maize.

'Tall' and 'minuta' seem to be a bit of a contradiction, but *T. minuta* can grow to a height of over 3 m.

Anyone who has smelt the khakiweed or the closely related garden marigold will instantly recognise the distinctive and clinging aroma. When maize for instance, is infested with this weed and harvested, the grain may become tainted with the smell. This can lead to the crop being downgraded with considerable financial consequences for the farmer. The smell has its benefits, however, as it is said to drive away nematodes. It has been suggested that the weed can be encouraged on fallow land and then ploughed in before a nematode sensitive crop such as potatoes is planted. An extract from the leaves of this plant is used in the perfume industry.

It is a weed that needs sunlight for germination, therefore germinating on or near the soil surface. This makes it susceptible to most pre–emergence herbicides as long as they do not leach into the soil. Even without soil disturbance the seed of khaki weed is able to germinate throughout the summer season provided it is not shaded by the developing crop. Best long season control is therefore often achieved with a herbicide programme that incorporates a post–emergence element. Cultivation will control the seedlings but will bring fresh seed to the surface where they will germinate.

ASTERACEAE

Taraxacum officinale
Common dandelion, Perdeblom

Height: 30 cm

Of European origin, the dandelion is now a common perennial weed throughout South Africa, being found on roadsides, in waste places and in gardens. It can be particularly troublesome in lawns and occasionally in maize under conservation tillage.

The leaves are used as a salad and the roots are used as a medicine. The roots can also be roasted and used as a coffee substitute when coffee is unavailable, as was the case during the World Wars.

Young plants are easy to control with post–emergence, systemic broad-leaf herbicides, but once established they become more difficult to control on account of their strong tap roots.

Tagetes minuta

Taraxacum officinale

ASTERACEAE

Tithonia diversifolia
Mexican sunflower, Mexikaanse sonneblom

Tithonia rotundifolia
Red sunflower, Rooisonneblom

Height: 1 – 3 m

Natives of South America, introduced into South Africa as ornamentals, these sunflowers are now widespread as weeds in the warmer regions of the summer rainfall area.

Reproduction is only by seeds, but they can produce perennial clumps that resist fire and contact herbicides.

They can grow up to 3 m tall and form dense colonies on roadsides, railway embankments and waste places, particularly in urban areas. *T. diversifolia* is especially common in Durban and Nelspruit, whereas *T. rotundifolia* becomes more frequent further north.

Infestations of these weeds not only cause serious and unsightly access problems, but they also totally swamp and replace the indigenous vegetation.

Control is best achieved manually, with chemical follow-ups, if necessary, on seedlings which reappear in cleared areas.

ASTERACEAE

Tragopogon dubius
Yellow goat's beard, Geelbokbaard

Tragopogon porrifolius
Purple goat's beard, Salsify, Persbokbaard, Wildeskorsenier

Height: 1 m

The goat's beards are semi-perennial weeds that are natives of Europe. They are now widespread in South Africa.

They are commonly found on roadsides, in waste places and old fields, mainly in the cooler areas higher than 1500 m above sea level.

They have a thick fleshy taproot and the purple flowered *T. porrifolius* in particular, has been cultivated as a vegetable. The roots are cooked in the same manner as a parsnip, which they somewhat resemble. They are closely related to the dandelion and like the dandelion, the whole plant exudes a white juice when broken.

No herbicides have been registered for these weeds, but they should respond to conventional industrial chemicals used on roadsides.

Tithonia rotundifolia

Tragopogon dubius

Tithonia diversifolia

ASTERACEAE

Tridax procumbens
Tridax daisy, Aster

Height: 25 cm

Originally from Central America, this annual weed was probably introduced to South Africa for cultivation as a useful plant in gardens, for soil binding and as a cover plant. It has escaped however, and is now a weed in the warmer sub-tropical areas such as the Natal coastal belt and the Transvaal Lowveld.

It is usually found on sandy soil on roadsides, in waste places and orchards.

Being a creeping stoloniferous plant, it is difficult to control once it has become established, especially in orchards. It seems to be tolerant to conventional weed control programmes. Best control would probably be achieved by first clearing established plants by hand and then using systemic chemicals on the regrowth.

ASTERACEAE

Verbesina encelioides
Wild sunflower, Wildesonneblom

Height: 80 cm

A native of South America, this annual weed was first recorded in 1934 where it was found growing on an old course of the Orange River near Prieska after a flood. It has since spread rapidly on sandy soil, especially on banks of rivers.

It is occasionally troublesome in croplands such as those in the Vaalharts Scheme.

There are no specific recommendations for its control, but it can be removed by cultivation whilst small.

ASTERACEAE

Xanthium spinosum
Spiny cocklebur, Boetebossie

Xanthium strumarium
Cocklebur, Burweed, Kankerroos

Height: 1 m

Both these species of burweed are widespread annual weeds in southern Africa, having been introduced from South America. Both species have burs that cause damage to sheep's wool. *X. spinosum* is somewhat less common and not usually found in annual crops, usually invading pastures and waste areas. It was the first declared noxious

Tridax procumbens

Verbesina encelioides

Xanthium spinosum

Xanthium strumarium

149

weed, when in 1860 the Cape government promulgated a law whereby the extermination of this weed was made obligatory under penalty of a fine (hence the well known Afrikaans name 'boetebossie' (bush for which one is fined)). It is still a proclaimed weed and should be removed by hand and burnt wherever it occurs.

The young plants are toxic.

X. strumarium is a common, poisonous and serious arable weed which is difficult to control. This is mainly because of extended germination from various depths and large seeds with large food reserves. It is a major pest of maize. All subspecies of *X. strumarium* are now considered to have originated from the same species, but there will be some variation from place to place.

Effective control is usually achieved with post–emergence herbicides and shallow cultivation during the seedling stage. There are nearly always escapes or late germinators, but these are usually shaded out by the crop. These escapes however, eventually form seeds which will maintain high seed levels in the soil once a field has become infested.

ASTERACEAE

Zinnia peruviana
Redstar zinnia, Wildejakobregop

Height: 70 cm

This plant is a native of South America and is now a widespread annual weed of waste places, roadsides and other disturbed areas. It has been regarded as a weed in South Africa for over a century.

It is not usually a problem, but if control measures are necessary, it should be susceptible to conventional herbicides and cultivation during the seedling stage.

BASELLACEAE

Anredera cordifolia (=Boussingaultia baselloides)
Madeira vine

Height: 1 – 3 m

Originating from South America, the Madeira vine has been cultivated in gardens and it is probable that from here it escaped into the wild. It is a perennial, succulent creeper that can grow over 7 m long, crawling along the ground and over crops, hedges and fences. The vine can produce seeds but is also spread by means of brittle underground, as well as aerial tubers.

Madeira vine is causing problems in the coastal regions of Natal where it is rapidly becoming a major problem in sugar cane. It is also troublesome in the Transvaal and in parts of the Cape such as Ceres, Cape Town and Tulbagh.

This weed is not susceptible to the conventional herbicides used in crop lands.

Zinnia peruviana

Anredera cordifolia

BIGNONIACEAE

Jacaranda mimosifolia
Jacaranda, Jakaranda

Height: 6 m

Introduced from South America in 1888, jacarandas, apart from being used as orna-mental trees, are also a widespread and invading weed.

A nurseryman named Templeman obtained the first two specimens from Rio de Janeiro and planted them in the garden at Myrtle Lodge in Sunnyside, Pretoria for a Mr Celliers. Myrtle Lodge is now part of the Sunnyside Primary School and these two trees are still there. Further seeds were imported and planted all over Pretoria and there are now a total of about 75 000 specimens, earning Pretoria the label of 'Jacaranda City'. There are also about 100 white jacarandas which originated from an individual specimen from Peru, donated in 1961 and which can now be seen in Arcadia Park.

Jacaranda, apart from being planted in towns and gardens throughout South Africa has invaded natural vegetation, especially along roads and watercourses. In these areas it is a highly undesirable plant because of its aggressive growth habit, replacing indigenous vegetation and consuming valuable soil moisture.

Jacarandas are very difficult to eradicate once established. Large trees must be ring–barked, cut below ground level or cut down and the regrowth treated with sys-temic herbicides.

BORAGINACEAE

Amsinckia menziesii
Fiddleneck, Vioolnek

Height: 1 m

Introduced into South Africa during the 1950s, probably from North America, this is now a weed of cereals in the Cape. The fiddleneck appears to be spreading into the O.F.S. and western Transvaal.

It is a serious weed of wheat in the Sandveld and on the sandy soils of the Swartland. Fine thorny hairs which cover the plant, cause severe discomfort at harvesting.

Fiddleneck is not adequately controlled by the hormone–type chemicals, but is suscep-tible to post–emergence contact herbicides and the sulphonyl ureas.

Jacaranda mimosifolia

Amsinckia menziesii

BORAGINACEAE

Cynoglossum hispidum (=C. enerve)
Hound's tongue, Ossetongblaar

Cynoglossum lanceolatum
Hound's tongue, Knoppiesklits

Height: 1 m

The two plants are closely–related and indigenous species that are widespread in the summer rainfall regions.

They are usually found in waste areas, along contour banks, roadsides and similar places.

The fruit of C. hispidum is borne on stalks up to 20 mm long, whereas those of C. lanceolatum tend to be smaller and on short stalks, (5 mm). The seeds, which are covered in tiny hooks, can stick to clothing and contaminate wool.

Both species are perennial plants, but reproduce only by means of seeds.

No specific herbicides are registered for the control of these plants, but they should be removed before they become established.

BORAGINACEAE

Echium plantagineum (=E. lycopsis)
Purple echium, Patterson's curse, Franklin weed, Pers-echium

Echium vulgare
Blue echium, Blou–echium

Height: 70 cm

These two species of Echium are natives of Europe and Asia and were originally introduced as ornamentals. They are now common weeds in South Africa as well as worldwide.

Purple echium is the most common and prolific, especially in southern Natal through to the north-eastern Cape where in spring, fields frequently turn completely purple. It is also a common weed of roadsides, orchards and vineyards in the Cape Province.

Purple echium has a strong tap root and large smothering leaves which can strongly compete with pasture crops for space and moisture. In a badly infested field the pasture will die from moisture deprivation whereas the Echium can flourish. It is well-known as a weed of pastures and lucerne in particular, being easily spread with contaminated seed or in hay used for animal bedding which is then spread in the lands.

Echium plantagineum　　　　　　　*Cynoglossum lanceolatum*

Echium vulgare

These weeds can be difficult to control. Herbicides must be used early in the spring before the plants are established or before commencing vertical growth. This is when the plants are small and susceptible to the chemicals but unfortunately, it is also when they are relatively small and insignificant that farmers tend to delay control measures until it is too late.

In Australia, where purple echium is also a major weed, work is under way to study the feasibility of biological control. (A man named Patterson was blamed for introducing *E. plantagineum* into Australia in 1880.)

BORAGINACEAE

Trichodesma zeylanicum
Late weed

Height: 1,3 m

Introduced from Europe and Asia this weed is now common in the northern regions, especially the northeastern Lowveld of South Africa and northwards into central Africa where it is a problem in cultivated lands.

It is commonly found on roadsides, waste places and orchards, becoming dense and competitive at times.

It is called 'late weed' because it germinates relatively late in the summer. It reproduces only by seed, but plants often survive for more than a year.

No herbicides have been registered for this weed. It should be removed when young since the mature plants have sharp hairs that can irritate the skin when pulled out by hand.

BRASSICACEAE

Capsella bursa-pastoris
Shepherd's purse, Herderstassie

Height: 40 cm

Shepherd's purse is a native of Europe, introduced to South Africa at the beginning of the nineteenth century, probably as a contaminant of crop seeds. It is now a common weed, particularly of vegetables, gardens and waste places.

Although occurring throughout the year, it is most noticeable in winter and of economic importance in vegetable crops grown in the winter rainfall area as well as irrigated crops elsewhere. It is an especially serious weed in wheat and other crops along the Orange river near Upington.

Shepherd's purse is known to be a secondary host to various *Brassica* diseases.

It is usually controlled effectively by herbicides and shallow cultivation.

Trichodesma zeylanicum

Capsella bursa-pastoris

157

BRASSICACEAE

Coronopus didymus
Carrot weed, Wild carrot, Swinecress, Peperkruid, Peperbossie

Height: 25 cm

Introduced from South America, this is now a common annual weed throughout South Africa.

It can become quite a problem in winter grown, irrigated vegetables, especially along the Natal escarpment. It is also well known in gardens, orchards and winter wheat.

Although generally growing fairly flat, it can become about 30 cm tall under favourable conditions and can create a tangled mass. The flowers are indistinct and produce what look like small bunches of grapes. These are in fact lines of paired seeds, which is where the name '*didymus*', being Latin for twin, comes from.

In maize lands winter weeds such as this provide cutworm moths with a place to lay their eggs, thereby increasing the potential cutworm problem the following season.

Coronopus is relatively tolerant to selective herbicides, especially those used in wheat. Particular care should therefore be taken with the choice and application of cereal herbicides; otherwise young plants are susceptible to most of the contact herbicides.

BRASSICACEAE

Lepidium africanum
Pepper cress, Pepperweed, Peperbossie, Sterkbos

Lepidium bonariense
Pepperweed, Peperbossie

Height: 1 m

L. africanum is an indigenous species whereas *L. bonariense* has been introduced, probably from South America.

The two species are very similar in appearance, the main difference being the shape of the leaves; those of *L. bonariense* having deeper marginal grooves and also tending to have larger seeds. They both have a sharp taste, hence the name 'pepperweed'.

Both species are common throughout South Africa and being frost resistant, often cause problems in winter crops. They are also common in many other situations.

Although usually annual plants, they may persist for two years and have strong stems which makes them difficult weeds to remove by cultivation once they have become established. Pepperweed is susceptible to most of the conventional herbicides.

Coronopus didymus

Lepidium africanum

Lepidium bonariense

BRASSICACEAE

Raphanus raphanistrum
Wild radish, Ramenas

Height: 1 m

Wild radish originated in Europe and is now widespread in South Africa, being the most important broad-leaf weed in winter cereals in the Cape. It is also a major weed of many crops in most other areas of the country. For example, in the north-eastern Cape it is a major problem in potatoes, in many areas of the country it is a weed of pastures and it is a winter weed in maize lands under conservation tillage.

Wild radish can be distinguished from similar weeds such as wild mustard by its deeply divided leaves and by the deep constrictions between the seeds. The seed 'pods' (not true pods but technically 'siliquae'), eventually break into single-seed portions. The flowers are variable in colour, often being white and even purple as well as the predominant yellow.

Not only is wild radish a competitive and unsightly weed, but it also harbours insect pests and diseases of crops such as cabbages and Japanese radish. Such crops close to fields full of these weeds often have problems with diamond–back moth and aphids.

It is susceptible to certain sulphonyl-ureas and to hormone-type herbicides but in sensitive crops, pre-emergence control is the best option. Wild radish is not controlled by the acetanelide herbicides such as metazachlor and acetochlor.

BRASSICACEAE

Rapistrum rugosum
Wild mustard, Wildemosterd

Height: 75 cm

Introduced from Europe and Asia, this plant is now a widespread weed in South Africa.

It is found in crops, orchards, waste places and roadsides, and can become dense and competitive if not controlled.

It can easily be confused with the various *Sisymbrium* species, *Erucastrum strigosum* and *Raphanus raphanistrum* or wild radish, but the 'pods' of *R. rugosum* have two segments: one making up the stalk, while the other is a terminal, globular seed. (These are not the true pods of legumes but are called 'siliquae'.)

As for most members of the *Brassica* family, *R. rugosum* is not susceptible to the acetanelide group of herbicides but is controlled effectively by the hormone-type and certain sulphonyl-urea herbicides.

Raphanus raphanistrum *Rapistrum rugosum*

BRASSICACEAE

Sisymbrium capense
Cape wild mustard, Strandwildemosterd

Sisymbrium orientale
Indian hedge mustard

Sisymbrium thellungii (=Brassica pachypodia)
Wild mustard, Wildemosterd

Height: 1 m

All these species are similar in behaviour and appearance to wild radish, *Raphanus raphanistrum*, and *Rapistrum rugosum*, which is also called wild mustard.

S. capense, which is indigenous, is not found in the Transvaal but elsewhere occurs throughout the summer and winter rainfall areas. It often becomes a problem weed in cereals, orchards and vegetables.

There are several weedy species of *Sisymbrium* of which the indigenous *S. thellungii*, with its relatively thick leaves and large 'pods' (siliquae), is the most common one. *S. orientale* from Europe and Asia, is now also fairly widespread. It has slender, rigid pods held away from the stem.

All of these weeds are found in crops, waste areas, orchards and on roadsides. The plants are edible when young.

Although these weeds are susceptible to the hormone-type herbicides, they are not susceptible to the acetanelide group, which are often used for broadleaf weed control in vegetable crops.

CACTACEAE

Cereus peruvianus
Queen of the night, Peruvian apple cactus, Nagblom, Bobbejaanpaal

Height: 6 – 7 m

Originally from South America, this cactus is now a serious alien invader in some parts of the Transvaal. It is especially prevalent north of Pretoria around Kameelpoort and towards Rustenburg and Groblersdal and also in Namibia. It is grown throughout the country as an ornamental and as a barrier plant and was probably first introduced as an ornamental.

Queen of the night is found mainly in the veld, growing under and among trees. It replaces indigenous vegetation and prevents animals from finding food and shade.

In spring it produces attractive white flowers; these flowers open mainly at night and close again the next morning unless it is cool and cloudy. The fruit are eaten by birds

Sisymbrium thellungii

Sisymbrium capense

Sisymbrium orientale

and monkeys thereby spreading the seeds. The seeds fall under the trees where the birds and monkeys sit, and land on a shaded seed–bed, which is ideal for the germination and growth of the cactus.

Chopped or broken branches are capable of taking root and forming new plants, so they should be buried deeply or burned. Pieces should not be carted away and discarded as this is one of the most common ways in which new infestations begin.

Small plants can be sprayed and larger ones injected with MSMA. They can also be chopped down, but the stem base must be dug up. It should then be deeply buried or burned.

C. peruvianus was proclaimed a weed in 1982. Every effort should be made to eradicate this plant, both on farms and in gardens whilst serious infestations are still relatively uncommon.

CACTACEAE

Harrisia martinii
Moon cactus, Toukaktus

Height: 1 – 2 m

Like the other cactus species (*Opuntia* spp.), the moon cactus also comes from South America, specifically Argentina. It is now found in Natal around Pietermaritzburg and in the Transvaal, especially in the thornveld around Pretoria.

It sprawls over valuable grazing in the thornveld and can climb over small trees, completely smothering them. It was declared a weed in 1968 but is still found being cultivated (illegally) as an ornamental in gardens. The small black seeds are favoured by birds and thus the weed is readily spread.

Moon cactus has been the subject of an intensive and successful control campaign that virtually eliminated it. However, in recent years it has reappeared as a problem plant and control efforts will have to be renewed. Chemical control is possible but as yet unregistered. Physical removal must be total as small stem sections can root and form new plants.

Biological control with a species of mealybug is proving to be successful.

Cereus peruvianus   *Harrisia martinii*

165

CACTACEAE

Opuntia aurantiaca
Jointed prickly pear, Jointed cactus, Litjiesturksvy, Litjieskaktus

Opuntia ficus-indica
Prickly pear, Turksvy

Opuntia imbricata
Imbricate prickly pear, Kabelturksvy

Height: 0,5 – 3 m

These 'prickly pears' are the more common ones of approximately eleven species that are declared weeds in South Africa. All of them are natives of the Americas. (There is only one indigenous species of cactus of any kind in South Africa.)

O. aurantiaca was originally introduced as a hybrid in the middle of the nineteenth century. It was planted for ornamental purposes in a garden in the Stockenstroom district of the Eastern Cape and was spread by missionaries to remote mission stations. It has escaped into the wild, becoming one of South Africa's most noxious and costly weeds. Jointed prickly pear is an inconspicuous perennial seldom exceeding 50 cm in height. The length of its joints and spines depend on habitat and climate. Its ease of spread, rapid growth and unpleasant spines result in infested areas rapidly becoming inaccessible, even to livestock. It is restricted to the Eastern Cape.

Each piece that breaks off the main plant is capable of rooting and producing a new plant. If the plant is cut down, all the pieces must be collected and destroyed. The seeds are rarely, if ever, fertile.

Chemical control is restricted to the spraying of MSMA. The introduction of cactoblastis as a bio-control agent has greatly reduced the problem. This is one of the finest examples of biological control of any weed.

O. imbricata probably found a use as a hedge and is more widespread.

O. ficus-indica can grow much taller and is well-known for its succulent fruit. It is found throughout South Africa. There are commercial plantations of this species and spineless varieties have been developed. Biological control with cactoblastis and cochineal has been partially successful. Chemical control is achieved with the injection of MSMA or glyphosate, but it is time-consuming and costly.

Opuntia ficus-indica

Opuntia imbricata

CACTACEAE

Pereskia aculeata
Barbados gooseberry, Lemon vine, Barbadosstekelbessie

Pereskia grandifolia
Large-leaved Barbados gooseberry, Grootblaar Barbadosstekelbessie

Height: 5 m

These succulent, perennial plants are from tropical South America and are planted as ornamentals. Despite being from the cactus family, they resemble bougainvillaea in habit.

P. aculeata has established itself in the wild especially in Natal, but is also found in other tropical areas where it invades natural vegetation, smothering indigenous species and restricting access on account of its unpleasant spines. The spines on the young growth are short and hooked and occur in the leaf axils. On old wood they are straight and occur in bunches.

P. grandifolia has not yet been recorded in the wild but has been declared a weed as a precautionary measure.

The fruits of the Barbados gooseberry are edible and the seeds are spread by birds and animals. It can form an impenetrable hedge and is planted for this purpose. The Zulu plant it over graves as protection against vandalism.

Chemical control is partially successful if the cut stumps are treated with a registered herbicide. All the cut pieces must be collected and burned as the succulent stems can take root if they fall onto the ground.

CANNABACEAE

Cannabis sativa
Indian hemp, Marijuana, Dagga, Isangu (Swati), Nsangu (Zulu)

Height: 1 – 2 m

A native of Asia which is now a cosmopolitan weed.

In terms of the Medical and Dental Pharmacy Act, 1928 (Act No. 13 of 1928) it is an offence to cultivate dagga in South Africa. Nevertheless it can grow and is grown in most areas and illicit trade in the drug continues.

The narcotic resinous substance is secreted by glands that are found mainly in the female flowers. Although the female flowers form the basis of the drug trade, the leaves can also be used. The female flowers occur on different plants to the male ones. The presence or absence of pollen is the easiest way of differentiating between them.

The weed is an annual, and if unattended, can grow to a considerable height (up to 4

Pereskia aculeata

Cannabis sativa

m). The seedlings are very distinctive, with one of the first two leaves being smaller than the other.

It takes approximately 80 man-days to pull up and destroy 1 ha of these plants after they have grown to a reasonable size. Manual eradication programmes are therefore laborious and expensive. Dagga is susceptible to the non-selective herbicides but must be treated at a young stage. If the plant is not killed effectively or sprayed too late, then tillering can occur, thus creating a denser and more prolific bush.

CAPPARACEAE

Cleome angustifolia
Peultjiesbos

Cleome gynandra
Spider-wisp, Snotterbelletjie

Cleome monophylla
Single-leaved cleome, Spindlepod, Rusperbossie, Enkelblaar-cleome

Cleome rubella
Pretty lady, Mooinooientjie

Height: 1 m

These species of *Cleome* are all indigenous.

C. monophylla is the most widespread and can be troublesome in field crops in all areas of the country. It can sometimes be quite a serious problem, as in maize in the northern and eastern O.F.S. and Transvaal, for example.

The seedlings can be confused with *Datura* spp. and with Crotalaria.

C. rubella is not as widespread as *C. monophylla*, being limited mainly to the western and north-western areas where it is a weed of summer grain crops.

C. gynandra is less common and only a weed of economic importance in the Northern Transvaal. It is cultivated by blacks as a spinach.

C. angustifolia is an occasional weed of roadsides and waste places, mainly in the Transvaal Lowveld.

The leaves of all these plants are edible and the seeds are sometimes used as mustard.

Cleome can be controlled by pre- and post-emergence herbicides as well as shallow cultivation when in the seedling stage.

Cleome monophylla

Cleome gynandra

Cleome angustifolia

CARYOPHYLLACEAE

Cerastium capense
Cape cerastium, Kaapse cerastium

Height: 25 cm

Cerastium is an indigenous species that is a widespread annual weed in South Africa but, as the name suggests, it is most common in the Cape Province.

It prefers damp, shady places and is often a nuisance in gardens and nurseries.

No specific herbicides have been registered for this weed, but it is easy to remove by cultivation.

CARYOPHYLLACEAE

Polycarpon tetraphyllum
Four-leaved allseed, Naaldvrug

Height: 20 cm

Of uncertain exotic origin, four-leaved allseed possibly originated from Eurasia. It is now common in parts of the Cape Province, the O.F.S. and Natal. It was first recorded in South Africa at the beginning of the nineteenth century.

It favours shaded places in waste areas, gardens and roadsides and has characteristic small white and green striped flowers.

There are no specific herbicide registrations but it is easily removed by cultivation.

CARYOPHYLLACEAE

Silene gallica
French silene, Gunpowder weed, Franse silene, Kruitbossie

Height: 50 cm

A native of Europe that has now become a cosmopolitan annual weed. It was introduced into South Africa at the beginning of the nineteenth century.

The plant is fairly widespread but is most common in the Cape Province, usually occurring in orchards and vineyards. It is an arable weed in East Africa.

It can become quite dense and competitive if left uncontrolled but responds well to both chemical control and cultivation when in the seedling stage.

Cerastium capense

Polycarpon tetraphyllum

Silene gallica

173

CARYOPHYLLACEAE

Spergula arvensis
Corn spurry, Sporrie

Height: 30 cm

Corn spurry is a major annual weed of wheat in Europe and was introduced to South Africa by Jan van Riebeeck as a fodder plant in about 1653. It is now widespread in South Africa being an occasional problem plant in pastures, cereals and gardens. It is a weak competitor and has not achieved the same pest status as in Europe.

Seeds excavated from Iron Age sites in Denmark, dating back 2 000 years, were found to be still viable.

Livestock and poultry are said to eat it readily.

Corn spurry is susceptible to pre–emergence herbicides, but effective wetting with post-emergence herbicides is difficult on account of the plant's fine, waxy leaves. This weed is well controlled by the sulphonyl urea group of herbicides and by heavy liming.

CARYOPHYLLACEAE

Stellaria media
Chickweed, Starwort, Sterremuur

Height: 40 cm

A native of Europe, chickweed is a common annual weed in gardens, particularly in damp and shaded areas.

It can form large mats with its sprawling growth habit. It is especially common in the Cape and can cause serious problems in wheat as it interferes with harvesting by clogging the combine harvesters. Because of the more favourable climate in Europe, it is generally a more serious problem in that region.

Chickweed is easily controlled by cultivation and is susceptible to many herbicides.

CHENOPODIACEAE

Atriplex lindleyi subsp. *inflata* (=*Blackiella inflata*)
Sponge-fruit salt bush, Blasie-soutbos

Height: 40 cm

Introduced, possibly from Australia, this perennial, semi-deciduous shrub is now a common weed in the more arid parts of the Cape Province and in Namibia.

Spergula arvensis

Stellaria media

Atriplex lindleyi subsp. inflata

175

It is commonly found in waste places and roadsides and can swamp indigenous fynbos once it has become established.

It is a short bush and the seed is contained in a characteristic balloon-like structure.

No specific herbicides have been registered for this species, but because of its perennial nature it should be controlled physically before it becomes established.

CHENOPODIACEAE

Atriplex semibaccata
Australian salt bush, Australiese brak(bossie), Kruipsoutbos, Brak

Height: 50 cm

Introduced from Australia at the turn of the century as a fodder crop, this plant is now common as a weed on disturbed ground throughout the coastal and dry areas of the Cape and up into southern Natal.

It is a perennial, woody and semi-deciduous bush when mature and not effectively controlled by contact herbicides. For this reason, it can be a problem in places such as orchards where these chemicals are widely used.

The Australian salt bush is readily grazed by sheep.

Control should be initiated when the plant is young and tender.

CHENOPODIACEAE

Chenopodium album
White goosefoot, Lamb's quarters, Fat hen, Withondebossie

Height: 1 m

C. album is of European origin and a common and important weed of many crops throughout southern Africa.

It is frost-tolerant and thus also well-known in winter crops, especially wheat in the O.F.S.

The seedlings appear furry on top and are often tinged with purple underneath. Under certain growing conditions the young plants turn bright purple in the centre. This contrasting green and red/purple colouring can be quite striking. Young plants are edible and the seeds are used to make flour.

C. album is easily controlled by cultivation and most of the pre- and post-emergence broadleaf weed herbicides; however, the waxy surface of the seedlings means that special attention should be given to post-emergence sprays.

Atriplex semibaccata

Chenopodium album

CHENOPODIACEAE

Chenopodium ambrosioides
Wormseed goosefoot, Kruiehondebossie

Chenopodium carinatum (=C. bontei)
Green goosefoot, Groenhondebossie

Chenopodium murale
Nettle-leaved goosefoot, Muurhondebossie

Height: 1,5 m

C. *ambrosioides* is from South America and a common weed of many warm countries. In South Africa it is widespread but usually found only on roadsides and in waste areas. It is common in Namibia.

C. *carinatum* came from Australia at the turn of the century and is widespread throughout South Africa. It is a serious weed of many crops, especially vegetables, in the Transvaal and Cape provinces.

C. *murale* is from Europe and very similar to C. *album*, which is also from Europe. C. *murale* tends to have a darker colour than C. *album*. It is of economic importance in irrigated vegetables.

There are several other exotic species of *Chenopodium* that are considered weeds.

All these species can easily be controlled by cultivation whilst they are still in the seedling stage. They are susceptible to many pre- and post-emergence herbicides.

CHENOPODIACEAE

Salsola kali
Russian tumbleweed, Russiese rolbossie

Height: 40 cm

Introduced from Asia, probably during the Anglo-Boer war, this is now a serious annual weed in parts of South Africa.

It is very common in parts of the Cape Province, Orange Free State and Namibia, being found mainly in waste places and on roadsides but also in orchards and gardens.

Russian tumbleweed is a very aggressive invader, being able to rapidly colonise new areas. As it is such a tough, unpalatable and unpleasant plant, it is a highly undesirable weed. Its only benefit is that it can act as an anti-erosion agent in bare areas.

The plant spreads easily by being broken off and rolled along the ground by a high wind, often for considerable distances.

This weed must be controlled whilst it is in the seedling stage.

Chenopodium ambrosioides

Chenopodium carinatum

Chenopodium murale

Salsola kali

CLUSIACEAE

Hypericum perforatum
St. John's wort, Tipton weed, Johanneskruid

Height: 1 m

This species is a native of Europe, Asia and North Africa and a weed of most of the temperate regions of the world. St. John's wort was originally introduced into South Africa in 1942 as an impurity in vetch seed that was sown at Helshoogte near Stellenbosch. Because of the ease with which it could spread it soon covered large areas of the south–western Cape. It is easily distributed by seed or the rhizomes which are often cut up and spread during cultivation.

St. John's wort has two distinct growth phases. In autumn and through the winter it is creeping and prostrate and in summer, it produces several woody, upright flowering stems. The stems produce flowers from November to January and die off towards late summer, leaving characteristic brown stalks.

It is poisonous to livestock, causing photosensitisation.

Biological control with a beetle was introduced in 1961/2. Periodic redistribution of the original beetles and further establishment of a gall midge have restricted the weed in most areas.

At present no herbicides have been registered for the control of this weed.

CONVOLVULACEAE

Convolvulus arvensis
Field bindweed, Akkerwinde

Convolvulus farinosus
Wild bindweed, Klimop

Convolvulus sagittatus subsp. *sagittatus*
Bobbejaantou

Convolvulus sagittatus var. *ulosepalus*
Wild bindweed, Wilde-akkerwinde

Height: 0,3 – 5 m

C. arvensis is from Europe and Asia and is distributed throughout South Africa and most other temperate countries.

It is a troublesome weed in cultivated lands and is difficult to control on account of its long underground runners. The runners can survive herbicide applications and even the most severe frosts. It can be differentiated from the morning glory by its arrow-shaped leaves as opposed to the latter's more heart-shaped leaves.

Hypericum perforatum

Convolvulus farinosus

Convolvulus sagittatus subsp. sagittatus   *Convolvulus sagittatus var. ulosepalus*

C. farinosus and the many subspecies and variants of *C. sagittatus* are indigenous to South Africa. All of them are difficult to control in cultivated lands, gardens and waste places. *C. sagittatus* var. *ulosepalus*, is a particularly serious problem in the wheat and vineyards along the Orange River.

Chemical control of these bindweeds is best achieved with systemic chemicals applied at the end of the growing season when nutrient movement is downwards to the roots and rhizomes. However, various cultural techniques can reduce the problem. Sheep will readily graze the foliage, for example, and pigs are fond of the underground parts. Lucerne can compete successfully with bindweed and to a certain extent can crowd out the roots. Repeated cutting of the lucerne also keeps the foliage in check.

CONVOLVULACEAE

Cuscuta campestris
Dodder

Height: 20 cm

This particular species of *Cuscuta*, which is the most common in South Africa, is in fact a native of North America. It has been known in South Africa for over 100 years. Dodder has a cosmopolitan distribution and is a noxious weed in Europe, Africa, Asia, Australia and Polynesia.

Dodder has no leaves or chlorophyll and is parasitic on a wide range of plants.

There are 17 indigenous species of dodder in South Africa. All of the plants are parasitic, attacking many crops. They are well-known as problem plant of lucerne and carrots.

Dodder is not controlled by the usual herbicides and the only successful method is to cut out and burn infected plants before they can produce seeds. The germination of dodder seeds is stimulated by the germination of the seeds of host plants in the soil nearby.

CONVOLVULACEAE

Ipomoea cairica
Coastal morning glory

Ipomoea coscinosperma

Ipomoea purpurea
Common morning glory, Purperwind

Ipomoea sinensis
Ijalambu (Zulu)

Height: 1 – 6 m

Some species of *Ipomoea* are indigenous, such as *I. cairica*, *I. sinensis* and *I. coscinosperma* and are relatively minor weeds. *I. cairica* has pink flowers and is common in the eastern

Cuscuta campestris

Ipomoea cairica

Ipomoea purpurea

Ipomoea sinensis

183

coastal areas up to the Lowveld. It is sometimes a problem in sugar cane, swamps and riverine vegetation along rivers such as the Crocodile river in Nelspruit. *I. sinensis* can be a weed of crops and gardens in sub-tropical areas. *I. coscinosperma* is an occasional problem on the Springbok flats.

I. purpurea, however, is a native of tropical and sub-tropical America and is a far more serious problem. It was cultivated as a garden plant and escaped, becoming an extremely troublesome weed in crops and gardens in most areas.

In frost–free areas individual plants of morning glory can survive from year to year and can reach enormous heights. In other areas, however, the weed is an annual. Its vigorous climbing habit can rapidly smother infested crops and interfere with harvesting by stringing all the plants together.

The flowers are usually purple or white, but occasionally have stripes of contrasting colours. The main leaves are heart-shaped, but the first two cotyledo-nous leaves are lobed. They are fine examples of how seedling leaves are sometimes strikingly different from the leaves of the mature plant.

The seed is said to contain a powerful hallucinogen. Maize grain is down–graded with only a small number of seeds present. The Zulus use the plant as a purgative and as an antisyphilitic.

Germination takes place over an extended period and from great depths. It is therefore not unusual for a maize crop in autumn to still have freshly emerging seedlings present, capable of climbing up the drying plants. For this reason it is an extremely difficult weed to control as it escapes most pre– and even post–emergence herbicide treatments. In some crops such as tomatoes, there are no selective herbicides that will control it. The morning glory is very sensitive to the hormone type herbicides, however.

CONVOLVULACEAE

Merremia tridentata subsp. *angustifolia*
Merremia

Height: 0,3 – 4 m

An indigenous plant that is common in the warmer regions, especially those of the eastern Transvaal.

It is a climbing, trailing plant that can be seen covering fences and other structures, especially in towns. This demonstrates its strong pioneering nature as it can grow in the dry bare areas along roads and fences. It can also invade old crop lands and orchards.

No herbicides have been registered for this weed, but it should be controlled before it establishes itself.

Merremia tridentata subsp. angustifolia

CRASSULACEAE

Crassula thunbergiana
Crassula

Height: 40 cm

There are over 350 indigenous species of *Crassula*, some of which become weedy. This particular one is an occasional weed of wheat in the sandy soils of the Cape.

This is a soft and succulent weed and should be susceptible to the herbicides normally used in cereals, although no specific herbicides are registered.

CUCURBITACEAE

Citrullus lanatus
Wild watermelon, Karkoer, Wilde waatlemoen

Height: 0,3 – 2 m

Wild watermelon is an indigenous annual plant that is a widespread weed in South Africa. It is found wherever the soil has been disturbed, especially in cultivated land.

It is not usually a serious weed, but because of its climbing growth habit, one plant can become large and competitive.

It must not be confused with the striped wild cucumber, *Cucumis myriocarpus*.

Because the seed of this plant is large and resilient, it can withstand many of the pre-emergence herbicides. Control is best achieved with post-emergence herbicides or physical methods.

CUCURBITACEAE

Cucumis myriocarpus
Striped wild cucumber, Streepwildekomkommer

Height: 2 m

An indigenous weed that is common in the summer rainfall regions of southern Africa.

It can become troublesome in a variety of crops on account of its tangled, much branched stems. The fruits are poisonous, but the leaves are eaten by blacks.

The striped wild cucumber must not be confused with *Citrullus lanatus*, the wild watermelon.

Because it is a deep germinator with large seeds, pre-emergence chemical control is not always successful. The weed can be controlled by shallow cultivation in the seedling stage. It is susceptible to post-emergence herbicides.

Crassula thunbergiana

Citrullus lanatus

Cucumis myriocarpus

EUPHORBIACEAE

Acalypha ecklonii
Acalypha

Height: 30 cm

The genus *Acalypha* has several weedy species of which *A. ecklonii* is possibly the most common. It is an indigenous plant that occurs mainly in the eastern parts of the country. It can reach a height of 30 – 40 cm and appears relatively late in the growing season in places such as maize fields.

Although quite common, as a competitor to crops, this weed is relatively insignificant and control would not normally be necessary. No specific herbicide has been registered for its control.

EUPHORBIACEAE

Chamaesyce hirta (=*Euphorbia hirta*)
Red milkweed, Rooimelkkruid

Chamaesyce inaequilatera (=*Euphorbia inaequilatera*)
Smooth creeping milkweed, Smooth prostrate euphorbia, Gladde kruipmelkkruid, Gladde–rooi–opslag

Chamaesyce prostrata (=*Euphorbia chamaesyce*)
Hairy creeping milkweed, Harige kruipmelkkruid

Height: 1 – 15 cm

C. prostrata and *C. hirta* are natives of tropical America, whereas *C. inaequilatera* is indigenous.

The main differences between the two creeping milkweeds is that *C. prostrata* tends to be hairy and have reddish stems, whereas *C. inaequilatera* has smooth and green or yellow stems.

Otherwise these two are remarkably similar in appearance, habit and distribution, which is widespread.

C. hirta is more common in the warmer, sub-tropical areas and has a more upright growth habit.

All three are annuals and exude a white latex when the stems are broken, as is the case with all *Euphorbiaceae*.

They are weeds of gardens and occur in bare exposed areas such as pathways, lawns and crops. The creeping milkweeds are sometimes a particular problem in citrus orchards, rapidly spreading onto the bare earth under the trees and competing for water and nutrients. Red milkweed is recorded as an alternate host to some important nematode species.

These weeds are easy to remove by cultivation and are susceptible to conventional herbicides.

Acalypha ecklonii

Chamaesyce hirta

Chamaesyce inaequilatera

EUPHORBIACEAE

Euphorbia helioscopia
Umbrella milkweed, Sun euphorbia, Sambreelmelkkruid, Son-euphorbia

Euphorbia heterophylla (=E. geniculata)
Wild poinsettia, Painted euphorbia, Wildepoinsettia

Euphorbia peplus
Stinging milkweed, Brandmelkkruid

Height: 0,1 – 1 m

E. helioscopia is a native of Europe that has been known in South Africa for over a century and is now widespread except in the O.F.S. Like all euphorbias, it secretes a white fluid when broken. This weed does not grow very tall (about 30 cm), but it can be moderately competitive if it becomes dense.

As it is well controlled by post-emergence contact herbicides, it is seldom a problem in situations such as orchards. However, in broadleaf crops this weed is less sensitive to the selective herbicides, thus posing a threat. The umbrella milkweed should be removed by shallow cultivation when in the seedling stage.

E. peplus, also originates from Eurasia and is a widespread annual weed except in parts of the Cape. It can cause skin irritations.

E. heterophylla is much more difficult to control and forms generally isolated but resilient populations in crops such as sugar cane in the sub-tropical regions of the country. These infestations should be removed by hand or spot-sprayed with systemic herbicides.

EUPHORBIACEAE

Ricinus communis
Castor-oil plant, Wonder tree, Kasterolieboom, Bloubottelboom

Height: 2 – 4 m

The origin of this species is not certain. It is probably from elsewhere in Africa and found its way here with Stone Age man possibly 3 000 years ago.

It is generally considered to be a perennial, although it is somewhat variable and a common weed of roadsides, waste places and occasionally in perennial crops such as sugar cane. It can grow up to 4 m tall, hence the names referring to a tree.

Although castor-oil is extracted from the seeds of this plant, it has to undergo extensive purification before it is safe for consumption. The seeds are extremely toxic to humans and animals, one seed being potentially fatal. The Zulus, however, use a paste for toothache and as a purgative.

Large plants can easily be controlled by chopping them out. The weed is generally sensitive to herbicides.

Euphorbia heterophylla

Euphorbia helioscopia

Euphorbia pepus

Ricinus communis

191

FABACEAE

Acacia dealbata
Silver wattle, Silwerwattel

Acacia decurrens
Green wattle, Groenwattel

Acacia mearnsii
Black wattle, Swartwattel

Height: 5 m

These are three species of 'wattle', that originate from Australia and are now serious invaders of veld, indigenous bush, watercourses, roadsides and occasionally, perennial crops such as sugar cane.

Originally, the black wattle was introduced to Natal in the 19th century by an immigrant named John Vanderplank who planted seeds from Tasmania on his farm at Camperdown. In Tasmania, wattles were used as windbreaks. Sir George Sutton of Howick, who noticed a secretion from the trees, sent a sample to England for analysis. Twelve years later, in 1889 he published the findings which started the commercial planting of black wattle for the production of tannic acid. This is used in the leather industry and the timber is of value for pulp, firewood and the mining industry.

The black and silver wattles are the more serious invaders and may appear difficult to tell apart; the glands on the leaf rachis of silver wattle are evenly distributed whereas those of black wattle are irregular. The overall appearance of silver wattle is a light grey-green colour, whereas black and green wattle have darker leaves. Green wattle is not very common and along with silver wattle, was probably introduced by mistake. Neither of them is planted commercially.

Long-term control of wattles is difficult as they coppice easily and produce large numbers of seeds that can remain dormant for well over 50 years. These seeds are efficiently dispersed by water and their germination is stimulated by fire. A combination of chemical, mechanical and management techniques, including the use of competitive cover crops, is usually required for effective control.

FABACEAE

Acacia longifolia
Long-leaved wattle, Langblaarwattel

Acacia saligna (=A. cyanophylla)
Port Jackson willow, Port Jackson, Goudwilger

Height: 5 – 20 m

Two species of *Acacia* that are originally from Australia. They are now serious invaders of natural vegetation, especially in the Cape coastal areas and now increasingly, in Natal.

Acacia mearnsii

Acacia dealbata/mearnsii

Acacia longifolia

Acacia saligna

193

A. saligna was first planted in 1848 to stabilise the loose sand which threatened to cover the new road from Cape Town to Bellville. It is now found around the South African coast from the Orange River to Kosi Bay and has more recently spread inland. This acacia also thrives in Zambia, especially on mine dumps.

A. longifolia is also widespread with isolated populations occurring throughout the country. It is the only invasive wattle with finger-like flowers. It was first introduced in 1827 but it was not until 1945 that it was recorded as being a problem plant alongside rivers at Houwhoek and Mitchell's Pass. It favours moist sites.

They are both capable of coppicing, although *A. longifolia* does so only rarely. They produce large quantities of seed which are dispersed by birds, animals and by human activities. Germination is stimulated by the passage through the digestive tract and also by fire. The seeds can remain viable for a long time. Port Jackson willow seeds have even germinated in painted concrete walls.

Control of these weeds can only be achieved with a combination of techniques of which the use of herbicides is only one aspect. Chopping, burning and cultural techniques must all play a part so it is advisable to consult an expert before embarking on a control campaign.

In the coastal areas, *A. longifolia* is being successfully controlled with a gall insect that reduces seed set. (The galls can clearly be seen in the photograph). Unfortunately this method of control is much less effective in mountain fynbos. Attempts are being made to control *A. saligna* with a fungus from Australia.

FABACEAE

Acacia cyclops
Redeye, Rooikrans

Acacia melanoxylon
Blackwood, Swarthout

Height: 4 – 25 m

Like the other invasive wattles, these weeds are from Australia.

The seeds of both these species are black with bright red seed stalks. The seeds of the blackwood are smaller whereas the plant is considerably taller than the redeye.

A. cyclops is well established in Mountain and Lowland Fynbos vegetation groups throughout the Cape coastal region. It can be a tall tree or in the form of a shrub, swamping indigenous vegetation. *A. cyclops* was introduced and used with *A. saligna* in the second half of the 19th century to stabilise the shifting sands on the Cape Flats. Many farmers, especially in dry areas, value this weed as fodder despite its high tannin content and reports that it is toxic.

A. melanoxylon can grow up to 35 m and is found from the south-western Cape, through Natal and into the high rainfall escarpment areas of the Eastern Transvaal. It

Acacia cyclops

Acacia melanoxylon

produces excellent timber and was originally introduced and planted as a forest replacement species in the Knysna forest around 1856. When indigenous trees such as yellowwoods and black stinkwoods were cut down, they were replaced with blackwood. It is still used to make furniture, especially in the Knysna district. Unfortunately, it is an aggressive plant and can smother indigenous species.

Redeye rarely coppices but blackwood can regenerate from vigorous root suckers. They both produce large quantities of long-lived seeds that make a massive seed bank in the soil. Apart from birds and animals, the seeds are spread in sand taken from infested areas and used for building.

Successful long-term control requires a co-ordinated programme of physical, chemical and cultural techniques. Biological control by means of a beetle from Australia is progressing.

FABACEAE

Acacia pycnantha
Golden wattle, Broadleaf wattle, Goue wattel

Acacia terminalis *(A. elata)*
Elata wattle, Elataboom

Height: 20 m

Both these wattles were introduced from Australia.

In 1893, *A. pycnantha* was planted in an attempt to reclaim dunes at Port Elizabeth and the Cape Flats. These sites are still the foci of modern infestations.

Golden wattle has a high tannin content but a relatively slow growth compared to the species grown commercially for their tannin.

A. terminalis is also planted as an ornamental and is established in the wild in parts of the Western Cape.

Control of these plants requires a combination of chemical, physical and cultural techniques.

FABACEAE

Alhagi maurorum *(=A. camelorum)*
Camel thorn bush, Kameeldoringbos

Height: 1 – 1,5 m

A native of Eurasia that has become naturalised in parts of the Cape Province.

The camel thorn bush is thought to have first appeared at a horse station near Oudtshoorn during the Anglo-Boer War, which suggests it may have arrived as a conta-

Acacia pycnantha

Acacia terminalis

Alhagi maurorum

197

minant of imported fodder. The plant established itself in the area and is now found throughout the Little Karoo and parts of the Northern Cape.

It has a strong ramifying root system making it difficult to remove by hand. The flowers are borne directly on what appear to be green thorns, but are in fact spine-tipped branches.

The camel thorn bush has been the subject of an intense eradication campaign, which although drastically reducing the infestation, did not eliminate it. If the pressure of the campaign is not maintained, this plant could once again multiply and spread, threatening the indigenous vegetation.

A herbicide mixed with diesel is registered for the control of this weed but chemical control on any scale is laborious and expensive. Every effort should be made to keep this weed under control.

FABACEAE

Caesalpinia decapetala
Mauritius thorn, Kraaldoring

Height: 2 – 4 m

A native of India and Sri Lanka, Mauritius thorn has spread as a weed in the high rainfall areas of South Africa.

Occasionally, in the north-eastern Transvaal and Natal it is planted as a hedge around kraals where it soon forms an impenetrable barrier, hence the Afrikaans name 'kraaldoring'. It has spread along watercourses and has invaded natural forests.

The Mauritius thorn coppices when cut and trailing branches root where they touch the ground. Wider dispersal is generally achieved by means of the large seeds which are readily transported by water.

This weed can be controlled by a combination of chemical and mechanical means. Chemicals should be applied to small plants or to the regrowth of larger individuals that have been slashed down. Seedlings and saplings can be uprooted when the soil is moist. However, to prevent coppicing without the use of a herbicide, the entire rootstock must be dug out.

FABACEAE

Crotalaria sphaerocarpa
Wild lucerne, Mielie-crotalaria, Wildelusern

Height: 1,5 m

Wild lucerne is a very common indigenous weed in the western maize growing areas and is a serious problem, especially in maize.

Caesalpinia decapetala

Crotalaria sphaerocarpa

About 80 indigenous species of *Crotalaria* have been recorded in South Africa. Several of them are minor weeds and only *C. sphaerocarpa* poses a serious threat.

Seeds of this weed are poisonous with the result that contaminated maize grain is downgraded.

C. sphaerocarpa is difficult to control pre-emergence as it germinates over the whole season and is large seeded. It is both a shallow and deep germinator. The deep germinating individuals can escape conventional herbicide programmes and become a nuisance later in the season. It is not well controlled by pre-emergence herbicides and is tolerant to most post-emergence herbicides once it is past the seedling stage. Care should therefore be taken with both the choice and application of herbicides if this weed is to be controlled effectively.

FABACEAE

Elephantorrhiza elephantina
Elephant's root, Eland's wattle, Olifantswortel

Height: 50 cm

An indigenous, perennial shrub which is a common roadside and veld weed in the summer rainfall areas, especially in the more arid areas of the western Transvaal.

It is not palatable, said to be poisonous to livestock and can be a serious competitor for moisture in places where it occurs. It sometimes forms extensive and continuous stands thereby seriously reducing the carrying capacity of the veld.

It characteristically bears its flowers at ground level and has a large fleshy, red root.

There are no herbicides registered for this weed.

FABACEAE

Leucaena leucocephala
Leucaena, Stuipboom

Height: 3 m

A perennial shrub from South America that was introduced as a fodder crop and as a source of firewood. It is still considered valuable for these purposes and seedlings can be bought from nurseries.

If allowed to grow uncontrolled leucaena can escape into the wild, and become a problem plant. It is found as a weed throughout the sub-tropical areas especially in Natal. It is usually found in road and railway reserves, river banks and disturbed areas.

Control is achieved by cutting down the plants and digging out the roots. Chemical control is very difficult.

Elephantorrhiza elephantina

Leucaena leucocephala

FABACEAE

Lotus subbiflorus
Lotus

Height: 30 cm

This is probably a fairly recent introduction from Europe.

It is widespread in the southern and eastern Cape where it grows in dense mats in moist places. It causes particular problems in lawns as it can swamp many lawn grasses.

There are no specific recommendations for the control of this weed.

FABACEAE

Medicago laciniata
Little burweed, Klitsklawer

Medicago polymorpha (=M. hispida)
Bur clover, Rough medic, Klitsklawer, Growwe medicago

Medicago sativa
Lucerne, Alfalfa, Lusern

Height: 40 cm

These plants are natives of Europe and are now cosmopolitan annual weeds.

Although *M. laciniata* is similar to *M. polymorpha* in habit and distribution, it has smaller leaves and burs.

M. polymorpha has been known in South Africa for over 130 years and is fairly widespread. It is, however, most common in the Cape Province where it is a nuisance in orchards and other disturbed areas.

Bur clover is a good fodder plant as long as it is kept grazed so that the burs do not develop; otherwise they can become entangled in the wool of sheep.

Lucerne is a common fodder crop but is now naturalised on many roadsides.

They are easy to control with conventional herbicides or by cultivation.

FABACEAE

Melilotus alba
White sweet clover, Witstinkklawer

Melilotus indica
Annual yellow sweet clover, Eenjarige geelstinkklawer

Height: 1 – 2 m

These weeds are natives of Europe and Asia and have been known in South Africa for over a century. They are now widespread annual weeds, having escaped from cultiva-

202

Lotus subbiflorus

Medicago laciniata

Medicago polymorpha

Medicago sativa

Melilotus alba/indica

Melilotus indica

tion. They are found throughout the country in any disturbed ground.

These species are said to be an excellent green manure, a good fodder crop and are favoured by bees. The plants contain coumarin which has a very characteristic odour and which can taint the meat, milk and eggs of animals that eat them. Flour made from wheat contaminated with seeds can also become tainted.

These weeds are susceptible to many of the pre-emergence herbicides and shallow cultivation.

FABACEAE

Paraserianthes lophantha (=*Albizia lophantha*)
Stinkbean, Stinkboon

Height: 5 m

This plant was first introduced from Australia by Baron von Ludwig who planted it in his garden in Cape Town in 1833. It escaped and is now found along most of the Cape coastal region and many inland areas. It favours the southern slopes of mountains and is dense in such places as the DuToitskloof Pass.

It is an adaptable species and since it has successfully established itself in Cornwall, England, suggests that it has the potential to spread further in South Africa.

When the seeds are broken and moistened it produces an obnoxious odour, hence the name 'stinkbean'. It produces copious quantities of seed which are spread around by various means, including the transport of sand for building purposes.

The stinkbean does not coppice readily if burned or cut close to the ground and regeneration after fire is usually from seed. Long-term control will therefore require repeated follow-up operations.

FABACEAE

Prosopis glandulosa
Mesquite, Muskietboom

Height: 6 m

A native of north eastern Mexico and the south-western United States, mesquite was first introduced in 1897 in the Okahandja Experimental Garden in the then South West Africa. German settlers in the area planted it for shade and fodder and by 1912 it was recorded as having established itself in the wild. It was also recorded as being cultivated around Upington in 1900. Mesquite is now widespread in the Karoo and Kalahari thornveld. There are several other weedy species of *Prosopis* from North America but they are of minor importance.

Paraserianthes lophantha

Prosopis glandulosa

205

The plant is extremely tolerant of drought, high temperatures and over–grazing. It forms dense thickets thereby excluding natural vegetation.

Control is difficult because plants damaged by inadequate removal resprout from dormant buds just below ground level, resulting in a dense multi- stemmed shrub. There is at least one herbicide registered for use as a soil application, but if either chemical or physical means are used to control mesquite, follow-up treatments are always necessary. Research on bio-control by means of a beetle from Arizona, is continuing.

FABACEAE

Senna didymobotrya (=*Cassia didymobotrya*)
Wild senna, Peanut butter cassia, Grondboontjiecassia

Height: 2 m

Introduced from tropical Africa as an ornamental, wild senna has become naturalised in South Africa and is now a serious and invasive weed.

It is found throughout the summer rainfall regions, especially in the eastern areas. It is commonly found in disturbed areas such as roadsides and waste areas.

Wild senna is a semi-deciduous perennial shrub that only reproduces by seed.

No specific herbicide has been registered for this weed and it is best controlled manually.

FABACEAE

Sesbania bispinosa
Spiny sesbania, Stekelsesbania

Sesbania punicea
Red sesbania, Rattlepod, Rooisesbania, Brasiliaanse glorie-ertjie

Height: 2 – 3 m

S. punicea is a perennial shrub and native of South America which was probably introduced as an ornamental.

From 1960 to 1980 it spread alarmingly in most parts of the country and was declared a noxious weed in 1979.

Red sesbania is found mainly in permanently or seasonally wet places but is also able to establish itself in disturbed areas such as roadsides and refuse dumps. In South Africa it is distributed from the Cape through Natal to the Transvaal Highveld and Lowveld.

This plant is a deciduous shrub and is spread by seeds which are contained in a characteristic four-winged pod. All parts of the plant are poisonous but the seeds are par-

Senna didymobotrya

Sesbania bispinosa

Sesbania punicea

ticularly lethal to birds and sheep; as few as six seeds can kill a chicken.

Biological control of this weed by means of a beetle from Argentina looks promising, which is very fortunate as chemical control is rather ineffective and costly. Several soil, foliar or cut-stump applied herbicides have been registered.

From a distance *S. bispinosa* looks similar to *S. punicea*, but has cream and purple flowers and long thin pods. It is a biennial, but the bare dried plants are a familiar sight in winter. It is also exotic, probably originating from Europe or Asia.

In the Transvaal Lowveld, at the Loskop Irrigation Scheme and in Swaziland it is a weed of cotton, rice and other croplands.

Control measures should be initiated before the plant becomes established.

FABACEAE

Trifolium angustifolium

Trifolium repens
White clover, Witklawer

Height: 25 cm

T. repens is one of several clovers introduced from Europe and Asia as a fodder crop.

Although still valuable as fodder, many of them are now naturalised in South Africa and are common and widespread weeds, especially in lawns. *T. angustifolium* was introduced from Southern Europe before 1862 but is now found only in the Cape Province where it is very common on roadsides and is often mistaken for grass.

Most of the clovers, being annuals or biennials will require systemic herbicides for eradication. They are susceptible to 2,4-D but not to 2,4-DB. The latter is used in pastures for broadleaf weed control when the clovers are a desirable component.

FABACEAE

Vicia benghalensis
Narrow-leaved purple vetch, Smalblaarperswieke

Vicia sativa
Broad-leaved purple vetch, Breëblaarperswieke

Height: 1 – 2 m

Several species of vetch have been introduced as fodder crops, with these two in particular subsequently becoming widespread and potentially serious weeds.

The purple vetches are found throughout the country, but especially in the winter rainfall region and in irrigated winter crops of the summer rainfall regions.

Trifolium angustifolium   *Trifolium repens*

Vicia benghalensis

Vicia sativa

They are primarily annual plants, but can survive for more than one season. *V. benghalensis* has a long group of flowers on a stalk whereas *V. sativa* has a solitary flower in the axils of the leaves. Despite their names, the leaves look similar.

Because of an extended germination period these vetches can often escape pre-emergence herbicides. They are, however, very susceptible to the hormone-type herbicides and continued use of these chemicals has substantially reduced the status of these plants as weeds.

FUMARIACEAE

Fumaria muralis (=*F. officinalis*)
Drug fumitory, Fumitory, Duiwekerwel

Height: 50 cm

A native of Europe which is now a widespread annual weed in South Africa.

Fumitory is troublesome in wheat, particularly in the eastern Transvaal and the Cape. It is also common in lucerne and many vegetable crops in the winter rainfall region, sometimes becoming-dense and competitive.

It is relatively tolerant to some herbicides, particularly in cereals and care must be taken to cultivate or apply herbicides before the plants become well established. Seedlings are more susceptible to the various herbicides than mature plants.

GERANIACEAE

Erodium chium

Erodium moschatum
Musk heron's bill, Turknael

Height: 20 cm

E. moschatum was introduced from Europe by the early settlers. It has been a common weed in the south and south-western coastal areas of the Cape Province for more than a century. It is found in orchards, vineyards, cereals, gardens and all disturbed areas.

It gives off a musk-like odour when crushed but is still eaten by sheep, goats and ostriches. However, where these plants are found adjacent to the coast it is thought that the odour becomes too strong with the result that livestock will not eat them.

E. chium is an indigenous species found over the same range.

These weeds are controlled effectively by shallow cultivation during the seedling stage and by most broadleaf herbicides.

Fumaria muralis

Erodium moschatum

ILLECEBRACEAE

Scleranthus annuus
Annual scleranthus, Knawel

Height: 20 cm

Annual scleranthus is a native of Europe that was introduced into South Africa in the nineteenth century and is now a widespread annual weed.

It occurs throughout the country but is most troublesome in wheat-lands and vineyards in the Cape. It is also occasionally a problem in vegetable crops, particularly onions.

It is a weak competitor and rarely requires specific control measures.

This weed can be controlled by shallow cultivation during the seedling stage and is susceptible to conventional herbicides.

LAMIACEAE

Leonotis leonurus
Wild dagga, Lion's ear, Wildedagga

Leonotis ocymifolia
Rock dagga, Klipdagga

Height: 2 m

These indigenous plants are commonly planted as ornamentals on account of their attractive orange flowers.

L. ocymifolia has smaller leaves than *L. leonurus* and the leaves of both species are sometimes used instead of tobacco. Despite this use and the common names, there is no evidence that the plants contain any intoxicating substances.

They are common as weeds of wasteland, roadsides and occasionally cropland.

They should be controlled when small.

LAMIACEAE

Ocimum canum (*=O. americanum*)
Hoary basil

Height: 40 cm

A plant of uncertain origin, but probably indigenous. Hoary basil is a common weed in the warmer parts of South Africa from Namibia, Northern Transvaal and down to the Natal Coast.

Scleranthus annuus

Leonotis leonurus

Leonotis sp.

Ocimum canum

213

The plants tend to spread on overgrazed or disturbed areas and are sometimes a nuisance in citrus orchards. This species is usually considered to be an annual despite being able to survive for more than one year.

The leaves have a smell when crushed, the strength of which varies considerably. In Namibia they are eaten and also dried and smoked as a cure for various chest complaints.

There are no specific herbicide registrations but control measures should be taken when the plants are still young.

LAMIACEAE

Salvia reflexa
Mintweed

Salvia stenophylla
Wild sage, Wildesalie

Salvia verbenaca
Salvia, Wild clarry, Salie

Height: 50 cm

Mintweed, which was probably introduced as an ornamental, is an annual from North America. The other two are probably indigenous.

These are common weeds of roadsides, waste places and occasionally pastures and croplands.

They can survive from one season to the next, but only reproduce by seed. Members of this family have a very distinctive and pungent smell and are said to taint the milk of cattle that have eaten them.

They should be controlled while small when they are susceptible to cultivation and conventional herbicides.

MALVACEAE

Abutilon sonneratianum
Wild hibiscus, Wildemalva

Height: 1 m

An indigenous perennial weed that is fairly widespread in the warmer areas of the Cape, Transvaal and Natal. It does not usually invade crop land but is found on roadsides, in waste places and orchards. It is especially common on road verges in the Pongola area in Natal and the eastern Transvaal Lowveld.

No herbicides have been registered for the control of this weed.

Salvia stenophylla

Salvia reflexa

Salvia verbenaca

Abutilon sonneratianum

215

MALVACEAE

Hibiscus cannabinus
Kenaf, Wild stockrose, Wildestokroos

Hibiscus trionum
Bladder hibiscus, Bladder weed, Terblansbossie

Height: 1 – 2 m

Two closely related annual species that are common throughout South Africa. *H. cannabinus*, however, is more common in the northern and eastern areas and is not found in the Cape Province. It was originally introduced from Asia as a fibre crop, the fibre being a substitute for hemp. Improved varieties grown in India are referred to as kenaf.

The hairs on the stem of *H. cannabinus* cause nasty irritations if one attempts to hold the stem with a bare hand or use a combine harvester to cut an infested crop.

The indigenous *H. trionum* does not possess the unpleasant hairs of *H. cannabinus* and has a flatter, spreading growth habit.

The fruits of these weeds are bladdery and contain the seeds. The leaves of *H. cannabinus* are more finely divided than those of *H. trionum* and are similar to the leaves of cannabis or 'dagga' with which it must not be confused.

Of the two species, *H. cannabinus* is taller, more aggressive and competitive. It is also a deep germinator and therefore less susceptible to pre-emergence herbicides. More reliable control can be obtained with post-emergence chemicals. *H. trionum* is relatively easy to control.

MALVACEAE

Lavatera arborea
Tree mallow, Mak-kissieblaar, Boommalva

Height: 2 – 3 m

Introduced from Europe and Asia, this plant is now a widespread weed in South Africa, especially in the south-western Cape.

It looks very similar to the small mallow, *Malva parviflora*, but it is much taller and has larger flowers; (the tree mallow can easily reach 3 m in height). For this reason it was probably originally planted as an ornamental.

It is a biennial and is usually found in waste areas and on roadsides, obstructing vision and appearing generally unsightly.

Hibiscus cannabinus

Lavatera arborea

Hibiscus trionum

217

MALVACEAE

Malva parviflora
Small mallow, Bread-and-cheese, Kiesieblaar, Kasies

Height: 0,5 – 1,5 m

This exotic weed originated in Europe and Asia and is now widespread in South Africa. It was possibly first introduced by early settlers for medicinal purposes.

It can now be found in all areas where it is usually seen on roadsides and in waste places. However, in the Cape it is a serious competitive weed of orchards and vineyards which, under favourable conditions can grow into quite a large bush. It has small, inconspicuous white or pink flowers.

If eaten in sufficient quantities it is known to be poisonous to livestock and in particular horses, especially after exercise. If hens eat it, it is said to cause pink yolks in the eggs. Blacks eat the weed with no apparent ill effects.

It is a perennial plant with the aerial parts being annual. For this reason it can be easily controlled with contact herbicides if it is sprayed while still young. Large, established plants will require a systemic chemical for effective long-term control.

MALVACEAE

Malvastrum coromandelianum
Prickly malvastrum

Height: 60 cm

This is a variable perennial or annual weed, native to North America.

Malvastrum is a common and sometimes serious weed of roadsides, orchards, waste places and perennial crops in the summer rainfall region, with the exception of the O.F.S. It is very drought resistant so it can be found growing on dry road shoulders where other weeds may perish.

Despite the name it does not actually have any thorns or prickles but is rather tough and leathery. It must not be confused with *Sida cordifolia* which it resembles strongly.

There are no herbicides registered for the control of this weed. It is probably susceptible to conventional herbicides, but only if it is sprayed when young. The seedlings can be removed by shallow cultivation.

Malva parviflora

Malvastrum coromandelianum

MALVACEAE

Modiola caroliniana
Red-flowered mallow

Height: 30 cm

This weed is a native of the Americas that is now common in South Africa, especially the summer rainfall region. It is a sprawling, stoloniferous creeper and was probably introduced as an ornamental. It is now found mainly in waste places and in gardens.

No herbicides have been registered for use on this particular weed.

MALVACEAE

Sida alba
Spiny sida, Stekeltaaiman

Sida cordifolia
Flannel weed, Heart–leaf sida, Hartblaartaaiman, Verdompsterk

Sida rhombifolia
Arrow-leaf sida, Pretoria sida, Smalblaartaaiman, Taaiman

Sida spinosa
Spiny sida

Height: 1 m

Even though these weeds are found in other tropical countries, they are, with the possible exception of *S. alba*, indigenous to South Africa and are found virtually throughout the country. (There is some doubt about the origin of *S. alba*, some authorities maintaining that it is indigenous, while some are of the opinion that it comes from Asia.)

Do not confuse Sida with *Malvastrum coromandelianum*.

These are perennial shrubs that grow up to about 1 m tall. They are characterised by their very strong tap root and stem that makes them almost impossible to pull up and tolerant to even the heaviest discing. *S. spinosa* is very similar to *S. rhombifolia* except for a short blunt spine at the junction of the leaf stalk and stem.

Being perennial weeds, these plants do not often infest annual crops, being more weeds of orchards, gardens, roadsides and old lands etc., but are well-known in cotton.

The very strong bark is used by some blacks as rough cordage.

The sidas are difficult to control on account of their physically resilient nature. They can be controlled by cultivation in the seedling stage but, when mature, they require systemic herbicides which can translocate to the roots. Pre-emergence herbicides give erratic control.

Sida spinosa

Modiola caroliniana

Sida rhombifolia

221

MELIACEAE

Melia azedarach
Syringa, Sering(boom), Bessieboom

Height: 3 – 7 m

The syringa is native to a large area extending from India to Australia and is now nat-uralised throughout southern Africa. It was first recorded as naturalised in 1894 in Natal.

It is a deciduous tree that is commonly found along streams, on railway embankments and in waste areas. It establishes itself easily in such areas, where it replaces indige-nous vegetation, blocks views and waterways, and is generally unsightly.

It produces an abundance of marble-size, pale yellow berries which, although consid-ered poisonous, are spread by birds, animals, water and human activities. These berries often remain on the tree for a year or longer.

The syringa coppices strongly, even from stumps that are cut to ground level and burned. For this reason it is very difficult to control. Physical removal of the stump and roots is effective but laborious and expensive. Ringbarking and bark-stripping usually stimulates coppicing and the development of root suckers. Trees should be cut well below ground level to prevent this.

There is at least one herbicide registered for use as a basal stem treatment. This prod-uct is mixed with diesel oil and painted onto the stem and stump. In order to get maxi-mum coverage, it is important not to cut the tree down too close to the ground. It is also important to make annual follow-up treatments in order to destroy escaped indi-viduals and seedlings.

MESEMBRYANTHEMACEAE

Carpobrotus edulis
Sour fig, Hotnotsvy, Strandvy

Height: 30 cm

Sour fig is an indigenous, perennial succulent that occurs throughout the Cape Province, especially in the east.

Many 'vygies' are toxic, but this one produces an edible fruit which is sourish in taste and eaten raw, preserved, dried or as a jam. Sour fig also makes a first class syrup and is said to be a laxative

Occurring on banks and roadsides, this plant can become weedy when it encroaches on such places as orchards and gardens.

No herbicides have been registered for the control of this plant.

Melia azedarach

Carpobrotus edulis

223

MOLLUGINACEAE

Gisekia pharnacioides
Gisekia

Height: 50 cm

An indigenous, annual plant that is an occasional weed in crops and gardens.

It is found in the summer rainfall regions, mainly in the warmer areas and is often found in sugar cane. It rarely becomes dense or competitive.

Gisekia is susceptible to the usual herbicides, especially those used in sugar cane.

MYRTACEAE

Leptospermum laevigatum
Australian myrtle, Australiese mirteboom

Height: 2 – 8 m

This weed was introduced from Australia as a hedge or windbreak, with the first recorded sighting having been made in 1850 from the White Sands plantation near Cape Town.

This plant has since become naturalised in South Africa and is found in patches on sandy soils from the south-western Cape as far east as Port Elizabeth.

It has distinctive seed capsules and the mature stems are twisted, furrowed and with ribbony bark. The plant also has strong lateral roots that produce a mat of tiny rootlets in the top 5 cm of the soil. These rootlets are so efficient at extracting moisture from the soil surface that other plants cannot compete. The Australian myrtle can quickly form dense thickets that threaten the flora and fauna of the Cape Province since no indigenous birds are known to nest in the shrub.

It is killed by fire and does not coppice if it is cut at ground level. However, fire stimulates the release of the seeds with a consequent massive germination after a fire has been through an area. Since it takes about four years before seeds are produced, follow-up burns for the seedlings need to be done only after four years.

Several soil-applied herbicides have been registered for the control of this weed. These are applied at the base of standing plants and eliminate the need for chopping or using fire.

MYRTACEAE

Psidium guajava
Guava, Wildekoejawel, Koejawel

Height: 2 – 3 m

A native of South America, the guava was brought to South Africa to be grown as an agricultural crop. It has now established itself in the wild and has become a serious weed.

Leptospermum laevigatum

Gisekia pharnacioides

Psidium guajava

It is grown as a sub-tropical crop and is found growing wild in all sub-tropical areas especially in Zululand and the Transvaal Lowveld. It can be found growing wild wherever the soil has been disturbed.

The fruit is eaten by a wide range of birds and animals (including man), which disseminates the seeds and assists in the spread of the weed. The guava is a host for fruit flies and wild bushes can act as a source of infestation of fruit flies to orchards of other fruit.

Once it has become established, the guava is extremely difficult to control. It is an evergreen, perennial plant with a strong root system, being able to withstand many foliar and soil-applied herbicides. It coppices when cut and produces vigorous root suckers. Ringbarking, bark-stripping and felling can encourage root sucker development and thereby a greater density of the infestation. It is best controlled by total removal of the roots or efficient use of a registered herbicide, if and when such registrations are obtained.

NYCTAGINACEAE

Boerhavia diffusa
Spiderling

Boerhavia erecta
Erect spiderling, Regopboerhavia

Height: 30 cm

The spiderlings are exotic, annual weeds from South America which are now common, especially in the warmer, northern areas of South Africa, however, they are frequently found in all areas.

The main difference between the two species is that the fruit of *B. diffusa* are sticky to the touch while those of *B. erecta* are not.

They are found in most situations, including croplands and gardens, frequently becoming a nuisance.

Spiderlings are susceptible to the usual herbicides.

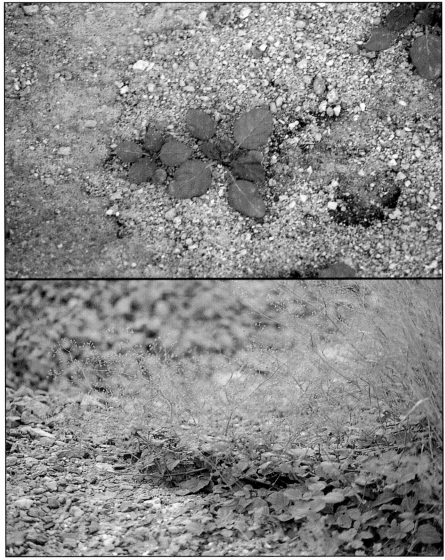

Boerhavia erecta

ONAGRACEAE

Oenothera biennis
Common evening primrose, Gewone nagblom

Oenothera indecora
Evening primrose, Nagblom

Oenothera jamesii
Giant evening primrose, Reusenagblom

Oenothera rosea
Rose evening primrose, Pienkaandblom

Oenothera stricta
Evening primrose, Nagblom

Oenothera tetraptera
White evening primrose, Witnagblom

Height: 0,5 – 2 m

The above plants are just a few of the 12 species of evening primrose that have been introduced to South Africa from the Americas, probably as ornamentals. Most of them come from Central America and have been known as weeds since the end of the 19th century.

They are biennials or perennial.

They are commonly found on roadsides in waste areas, old lands and occasionally in crops, especially when under conservation tillage. *O. indecora* and *O. stricta* are serious weeds in orchards and vineyards in the Cape.

They are called evening primroses because of their habit of opening just before sunset and closing again before noon the following day. The flowers vary in colour and some of the yellow species turn pink as they age. They have a thick, stubby tap root.

The plants are controlled by cultivation when still small and are generally susceptible to contact herbicides when they are seedlings. Once they have become established, however, they become tolerant to most chemicals, therefore control must be initiated early.

Oenothera tetraptera

Oenothera stricta

Oenothera rosea

Oenothera indecora

Oenothera jamesii

OXALIDACEAE

Oxalis corniculata (=*O. repens*)
Creeping sorrel, Tuinranksuring

Oxalis latifolia
Red garden sorrel, Rooituinsuring

Oxalis pes-caprae
Yellow sorrel, Geelsuring

Oxalis purpurea
Sorrel, Suring

Height: 25 cm

There are approximately 500 species of *Oxalis*, many of which (about 243), occur in South Africa. The majority of these plants are found only in the Cape. The sorrels mentioned here are those which commonly occur as weeds and they are widespread throughout South Africa.

Creeping sorrel is from Europe and red sorrel from South America, while the others are indigenous. It is significant that of all the species of *Oxalis* that occur in South Africa, the two that are not indigenous are two of four that are considered troublesome weeds.

Red and yellow sorrel have bulbs, whereas creeping sorrel has underground stolons. They all survive as perennials by means of these underground parts.

Creeping sorrel is a problem of lawns and gardens as well as crops and orchards, but the others, especially *O. latifolia* are more common in cultivated crops.

The sorrels sometimes contain enough oxalic acid to cause poisoning in livestock. They can also act as hosts for plant diseases such as various kinds of rust.

Yellow sorrel in particular, has pleasantly acid-tasting leaves and is sometimes added to salads. The bulbs are edible and in the past were used as a vermifuge.

The sorrels are not very competitive and do not usually cause crop losses. They are, however, very difficult to eradicate as the bulbs or stolons are very tolerant to herbicides even though surface growth can be controlled easily with 2,4-D and other hormone herbicides. If attempts are made to dig them up, all the bulblets or stolons must be removed to prevent regeneration. It is claimed that creeping sorrel in lawns can be controlled by an application of lime. It is known however, that the plant is intolerant of alkaline conditions.

Oxalis corniculata

Oxalis latifolia

Oxalis pes-caprae

Oxalis purpurea

PAPAVERACEAE

Argemone mexicana
Yellow-flowered Mexican poppy, Geelblombloudissel

Argemone ochroleuca (=A. *subfusiformis*)
White-flowered Mexican poppy, Mexikaanse papawer

Height: 1 m

The Mexican poppies are of South American origin and are now widespread in South Africa. Because of their pioneering natures they were not originally declared noxious weeds, although many weeds (which are all usually pioneers) have since been proclaimed. Pioneer plants often help to prevent erosion as they are usually the first plants to become established on bare ground. These particular weeds are often found on recently cleared sites, new dam walls etc. as well as many crops.

The flowers of these weeds look like typical poppies, but because of their spiny leaves, they are often mistaken for thistles. They have been suspected of causing poisoning of humans and the seeds contaminate sheep's wool. When cut, the plants exude a yellow latex and have a distinctive odour when crushed. In maize lands they may appear late in the season, particularly in the western maize areas. They are sometimes a problem in wheat.

Mexican poppies are usually controlled effectively by shallow cultivation. When small, most post-emergence herbicides can be used to control them.

PAPAVERACEAE

Papaver aculeatum
Wild poppy, Thorny poppy, Koringpapawer, Doringpapawer

Papaver rhoeas
Field poppy, Koringpapawer

Height: 75 cm

The wild poppy is indigenous, whereas the field poppy was introduced to South Africa from Europe, being the same species common in the crops and old battlefields of northern France. They were first planted in South Africa as ornamentals.

Both species are annuals.

P. aculeatum, with an orange or salmon–coloured flower and spiny stems, is widespread in South Africa. It is mainly a weed of old lands, waste places and roadsides. *P. rhoeas*, which has a red flower is a weed of wheat in parts of the Cape Province.

There are no specific herbicides registered for these weeds, but being small-seeded, shallow germinators they should be susceptible to chemicals and cultivation during the seedling stage.

Argemone mexicana

Papaver aculeatum

Argemone ochroleuca

233

PASSIFLORACEAE

Passiflora subpeltata
Wild grenadilla, Wildegrenadella

Height: 4 m

One of several species of *Passiflora* that are natives of South America. They were probably introduced as climbing ornamentals or, like the passion fruit, for the fruit. They have now spread into various niches in most areas of the country.

This particular species is common in the forests of the Natal Midlands, where it clambers over trees and saplings, interfering with growth and harvesting. It also occurs in the Transvaal.

The grenadillas are perennial plants and as such need to be controlled effectively. Systemic chemicals or total physical removal are the best methods.

PEDALIACEAE

Ceratotheca triloba
Rhodesian foxglove, Wild foxglove, Vingerhoedblom

Height: 1,75 m

An indigenous weed that is widespread in the warmer areas of the sub-continent from Natal to Central Africa.

It is common in disturbed areas such as roadsides, waste areas, fallow land and occasionally in grass and cropland. It can behave both as a perennial or as an annual and is sometimes cultivated as an ornamental.

The leaves have an unpleasant smell when crushed, sometimes described as being like the smell of crushed locusts.

No herbicides have been registered for this weed but it should be susceptible to chemicals and cultivation, especially when young.

PEDALIACEAE

Dicerocaryum eriocarpum (=D. zanguebarium)
Boot protector, Devil's thorn, Beesdubbeltjie

Height: 10 cm

An indigenous species that is common in the sub-tropical areas, occurring on roadsides, in waste areas and disturbed veld.

It has a thick, perennial, woody rootstock that produces annual stems that can trail along the ground for over 2 m. The hard spines on the fruit can injure animals' feet.

Passiflora subpeltata

Ceratotheca triloba

Dicerocaryum eriocarpum

When crushed in water it becomes slimy and soaplike and is used by blacks as a shampoo or soap.

This weed should be removed when young.

PEDALIACEAE

Sesamum triphyllum
Wild sesame, Thunderbolt flower, Wildesesam, Seeroogblaar

Height: 2 m

Wild sesame is an indigenous and widespread annual weed common throughout South Africa's summer rainfall region.

This weed occasionally becomes troublesome in crops in the northern and eastern Transvaal. It is also common along roadsides in Natal.

There are other, very similar species of *Sesamum*, but they must not be confused with *Ceratotheca triloba*.

This weed should be controlled when small.

PHYTOLACCACEAE

Phytolacca heptandra
Wild sweet potato, Boesmandruiwe

Phytolacca octandra
Inkberry, Pokeweed, Bobbejaandruif, Inkbessie

Height: 1 – 2 m

There are several species of *Phytolacca* occurring as weeds in South Africa. Most of them are natives of the Americas. *P. heptandra* is indigenous and most common in Natal and the Cape Province. *P. octandra* is probably exotic and occurs mostly in the eastern parts of the country. It was reported to have come into Natal when the railway cuttings between Durban and Pietermaritzburg were made in about 1865. Before this it was unknown in the region.

The Afrikaans names refer to the grape-like fruit which is favoured by baboons in some areas, even though they are said to be poisonous and capable of causing skin irritations. The seeds are efficiently dispersed by birds.

Phytolacca must not be confused with *Cestrum laevigatum*, which shares its common name. Inkberry is a major weed of forestry in South Africa as it rapidly invades clear-felled areas and can grow into quite a large bush. The inkberry also occurs on roadsides and in wasteplaces and gardens.

The weed is easily controlled by chemical or mechanical means, especially when small.

Sesamum triphyllum

Phytolacca octandra

PLANTAGINACEAE

Plantago lanceolata
Buckhorn plantain, Ribwort, Smalblaarplantago, Smalweëblaar, Oorpynhoutjie

Plantago major
Broadleaf ribwort, Rippleseed plantain, Grootweëblaar

Height: 45 cm

Collectively called plantains, these closely related species are natives of Europe and are now cosmopolitan. They have followed man's pioneering activities into the New World, being called 'White man's footprints' by the North American Indians.

They are widespread in South Africa and common along roadsides, on waste land and in gardens. They can become a problem in lucerne, clover fields and orchards, for example, with the seeds being a common impurity of grass and clover seeds.

P. major is shorter, with broader, ovate leaves as opposed to the long, narrow leaves of *P. lanceolata*. It also has a relatively larger group of flowers and is considerably less common than *P. lanceolata*.

The plantains are easily recognised by the compact, tough flower on the end of a long stalk commonly containing up to 1000 seeds. The pollen is a major factor in causing hayfever and the Afrikaans name 'oorpynhoutjie' refers to the old custom of placing small pieces of the inflorescence in the ear as a remedy for earache.

If they are sprayed at an early stage they are susceptible to post-emergence herbicides.

POLYGONACEAE

Emex australis
Spiny emex, Devil's thorn, Emexdubbeltjie, Volstruisdoring, Dubbeltjie, Kaapse dubbeltjie

Height: 40 cm

A weed that is indigenous to the Cape, but is now widespread in South Africa and worldwide. (*'Australis'* means 'southern', not necessarily from Australia.)

In cultivated land this weed is more important in the winter rainfall region but during recent years it has spread to irrigated and dryland wheat in the summer rainfall areas. Although the spiny emex occurs in wheat fields in the Orange Free State it is not an important weed in this region. *Emex* is now a serious weed in Australia having been accidentally introduced there from South Africa aboard early sailing ships crossing the Pacific on which it was cultivated as a source of vitamin C.

Emex is usually a spreading plant but when dense can grow to about 60 cm, becoming very competitive under favourable conditions and occasionally does become competitive in citrus orchards.

Plantago lanceolata

Plantago major

Emex australis

Male and female flowers are borne separately on the same plant at the base of the leaf stalk; these separate flowers are an unusual characteristic which is also well exhibited in maize. The seed, which is present throughout the year, has three strong spines and can injure the feet of bare-footed people and animals.

It is susceptible to shallow cultivation and conventional broadleaf-weed herbicides.

This dubbeltjie or devil's thorn must not be confused with the 'common dubbeltjie', *Tribulus terrestris*.

POLYGONACEAE

Fallopia convolvulus (=*Polygonum convolvulus*) (=*Bilderdykia convolvulus*)
Climbing knotweed, Black knotweed, Wild buckwheat, Wildebokwiet, Slingerduisendknoop

Height: 1 – 3 m

A native of Europe which is now a widespread and troublesome weed in South Africa, particularly in winter wheat and vegetables. It is especially a problem in the eastern O.F.S. and at the Loskop Irrigation Scheme. In Natal, it is a minor weed in Weenen and Winterton. It has probably been spread by contaminated wheat seed.

Black knotweed is a climbing annual with a deep tap root. The flowers, unlike morning glory with which it is sometimes confused, are small and green or white. The leaves are narrow and arrow-like and the fruits distinctly triangular. It is easily identifiable in its seedling stage.

The climbing habit of this weed means that it can grow above the crop canopy for sunlight and can easily smother the crop thereby affecting yields and interfering with harvesting. The fact that it is usually still green when wheat is ripe exacerbates the problem.

Black knotweed is relatively tolerant to some herbicides especially the hormone-type herbicides, so care must be taken with a suitable choice of chemical. Particular attention must be paid to correct and efficient application.

POLYGONACEAE

Oxygonum sinuatum
Oxygonum

Height: 50 cm

This plant is an indigenous and fairly widespread weed. It is most common in the subtropical regions where it occurs in disturbed areas such as on roadsides, in waste places and citrus orchards. It is an arable weed in East Africa.

The small white flowers and spiny fruit occur on a long leafless stem. The fruit can injure bare feet. It reproduces only by seed but plants can survive for several seasons.

240

Fallopia convolvulus

Oxygonum sinuatum

No herbicides have been registered for this weed. It is best controlled manually and should be removed before it sets seed.

POLYGONACEAE

Polygonum aviculare
Prostrate knotweed, Knotweed, Voëlduisendknop, Koperdraad, Litjiesgras

Polygonum lapathifolium
Spotted knotweed, Hanekam

Persicaria serrulata (=*Polygonum salicifolium*)
Snakeroot, Slangwortel

Naturalised from Europe, these annual weeds are widespread in South Africa. They are usually found on roadsides, in waste places, in croplands and in moist areas.

P. aviculare is a major weed of winter wheat and vegetables, particularly in the O.F.S. and Cape. In wheat, for instance, if conditions are favourable, it can clamber over the crop, severely reducing the crop potential and hampering the harvesting operation. It is usually recognized by its small pink flowers and is likely to sprawl along the ground in the absence of a dense crop.

The prostrate knotweed is difficult to control with some wheat herbicides as it has an extended period of emergence, adding to its status as a problem plant. Particular care must be taken with the choice and application of herbicides. Nevertheless, many farmers in the Cape value this plant as grazing after their cereal crop. 100% control is therefore not considered desirable, so they choose chemicals that are less effective and only suppress the weed.

P. lapathifolium, which gets its English common name from the distinct dark spots on its leaves, can tolerate very moist conditions. It is common on river banks, dam walls and can even grow in water.

The leaves of *Persicaria serrulata* are stalkless but otherwise its appearance and habit are very similar to *P. lapathifolium*.

No specific control measures are recommended for these weeds.

POLYGONACEAE

Rumex crispus
Curly dock, Krultongblaar, Wildespinasie

Rumex lanceolatus
Smooth dock, Gladdetongblaar

Height: 1,5 m

R. crispus is from Europe whereas *R. lanceolatus* is indigenous. They are both widely distributed in South Africa.

Polygonum aviculare

Polygonum lapathifolium

Rumex crispus

243

These two 'docks' are usually found in ditches and moist, waste places. They can become troublesome in orchards and vineyards, especially in the Cape.

The leaves of the dock are said to have medicinal properties. They are believed to relieve the pain of insect stings and bites, as well as the skin irritation caused by certain plants.

Because of their perennial nature, systemic herbicides should be used for the eradication of these weeds. In orchards and vineyards they respond well to systemic, non-selective herbicides.

POLYGONACEAE

Rumex acetosella subsp. *angiocarpus* (=*Rumex angiocarpus*)
Sheep sorrel, Rooisuring, Steenboksuring

Height: 30 cm

Accidentally introduced from Europe by early Dutch colonists, sheep sorrel is now a widespread weed in South Africa.

Sheep sorrel is a common perennial weed of cultivated lands and sometimes, because of its underground rhizomes, can become a serious problem. It is more of a problem on acid soils than in other soils. and is particularly troublesome in the Orange Free State and Griqualand East.

The weed can be controlled by correct management and pre- and post-emergence herbicides.

PORTULACACEAE

Portulaca oleracea
Purslane, Pigweed, Porslein, Varkkos

Portulaca quadrifida
Wild purslane, Porslein

Height: 15 cm

Purslane, *P. oleracea*, is a creeping, succulent annual, introduced from Europe during the early settler days. It occurs in all areas of South Africa, often growing vigorously into dense mats in crops and gardens.

The English name for this plant, 'pigweed', is confusing as various members of the *Amaranthus* family are also referred to as pigweeds.

P. oleracea has been implicated as a host plant for the overwintering of the pathogen that causes *Verticillium* wilting disease in cotton.

Because of their succulent nature and having large moisture reserves, the plants can

Rumex acetosella subsp. angiocarpus

Portulaca oleracea

Portulaca quadrifida

survive for some time after being uprooted or broken. Small pieces can then set root and produce new plants, especially under moist conditions. This makes it difficult to eradicate by cultivation.

Purslane is relatively easy to control with pre-emergence herbicides, as it is small-seeded and a shallow germinator. Good wetting agents should be used with post-emergence herbicides, however, to ensure good coverage and penetration of the waxy leaves.

P. quadrifida is a perennial and probably also exotic. It is not as common as *P. oleracea*, but is widespread in waste places and orchards in the summer rainfall regions. It has a distinctive red flower.

No herbicides have been registered for use on this weed.

PRIMULACEAE

Anagallis arvensis
Pimpernel, Bird's eye, Blouselblommetjie

Height: 25 cm

The pimpernel is an exotic annual from Eurasia that has been known as a weed in South Africa since the middle of the 19th century. It was introduced as a contaminant of crop seeds by European settlers.

It is usually found in damp situations, being capable of flourishing in lower light densities. It is common in cereals in the Cape.

The usual colour of the flower in Africa is blue, although red and pink forms do occur, especially in the Cape. In Europe, where the usual colour of the plant is red, it is called the 'scarlet pimpernel'. They are thought to be the same species.

Pimpernel is poisonous to birds and animals.

It does not often grow profusely, so specific control measures are not normally required. It, however, is easy to control by cultivation and it is susceptible to normal herbicides.

PROTEACEAE

Hakea gibbosa
Rock hakea, Harige hakea

Hakea sericea
Silky hakea, Needle bush, Syerige hakea, Naaldbos

Hakea suaveolens
Sweet hakea, Soethakea

Height: 3 – 5 m

These three species of *Hakea* were introduced from Australia in the 1830s probably for use as hedges and to control drift sand. They were well established in the Cape coastal

246

Anagallis arvensis

Hakea gibbosa

Hakea sericea

Hakea suaveolens

247

region by 1900 and at one time covered 4 800 km² or 14% of the Mountain Fynbos.

H. gibbosa, which is hairy and has very prickly leaves, and *H. sericea*, which is hairless and less prickly, are the major threats to the Mountain Fynbos. They can completely replace indigenous vegetation and make mountain slopes unattractive and inaccessible to mountaineers, promote erosion and increase transpiration, with subsequent reduction of run-off to rivers and dams.

H. suaveolens has divided and hairless leaves, shiny, warted and clustered fruits and flowers borne in catkin–like clusters. It is a weed of lesser importance.

The winged seeds are carried in fire-resistant structures called follicles, which will only open when the parent plant dies. When a fire passes through an infested area, massed release of the seeds is triggered. Old, dry hakea stands are extremely flammable and cause such hot fires that all indigenous flora and fauna in the vicinity are destroyed. These bare areas are quickly recolonised by the hakea.

Although biological control seems to be keeping these weeds under control, it may still be necessary to use other control methods occasionally. Plants should be cut off below the lowest leafy parts and then stacked to dry for 8 to 12 months. Each stack should be weighted down or anchored so that it cannot blow about, and be left until all the seeds have been released. Many of these seeds will be eaten by rodents but those that germinate must be killed by fire or other methods. A soil-applied herbicide has been registered but its use is risky and expensive.

No other herbicides have been registered for use on this weed.

RESEDACEAE

Reseda lutea
Dyer's rocket, Katstert

Height: 35 cm

Introduced from Europe and Asia, this plant is now a weed, especially in the Cape Province.

This weed is a perennial with a fleshy, tuberous root that survives the annual aerial parts. It can cause problems during the harvesting of cereals as it remains green and clogs up the combines.

Dyer's rocket is difficult to control and there are no specific herbicides registered for this weed. It does, however, appear to be moderately susceptible to the sulphonyl ureas that are used in cereals.

Reseda lutea

ROSACEAE

Agrimonia procera (=*A. odorata*)
Agrimony, Geelklits

Height: 1,75 m

Agrimony is a native of Europe that has become a widespread weed of Asia, North America and now South Africa.

It is a perennial plant although the aerial parts will die off in winter and regrow in the spring.

Agrimony is found throughout the more temperate regions of the country on roadsides in particular, but can often be seen invading grassland and perennial pastures.

The fruit are covered with hooked bristles that enable them to stick to clothing, hair and sheep's wool. Contaminated wool is downgraded.

As it is a perennial plant, it will usually require systemic herbicides unless it can be removed when still a seedling.

ROSACEAE

Rubus cuneifolius
American bramble, Sand bramble, Amerikaanse braambos, Sandbraam

Rubus rigidus
Bramble, Braam

Rubus rosifolius
Wild raspberry, Wildeframboos

Height: 2 m

There are several species of 'bramble' in South Africa, some being indigenous, such as *R. rigidus,* and some being exotic. There are many forms, hybrids and sub-species of bramble.

All brambles are perennial shrubs.

R. cuneifolius was introduced from North America at the turn of the century by a farmer who wished to make a living by making bramble jam. The American bramble is just one of the species that is now becoming a serious problem, mainly in parts of Natal, where it forms impenetrable clumps in the veld, on roadsides, and in forests. When ripe, the fruits are tasty and good to eat. The American bramble is closely related to the European species of bramble but has far more unpleasant thorns. Some cultivars without thorns and with large fruit have been developed and are grown commercially overseas for their 'blackberries'.

There are also various species of wild raspberry but these are generally not as invasive as brambles.

Agrimonia procera

Rubus cuneifolius

Rubus rosifolius

The bramble and raspberry are spread by seeds in the fruit which are eaten and dispersed by various animals, but by birds in particular. The small seeds in the berries have a hard, resistant seed-coat which ensures the survival of the seed through the digestive tract of birds, animals and humans. The bramble also spreads vegetatively by means of tip-rooting and sucker formation on the roots. Sucker development is stimulated when the aerial part of the plant has been destroyed by fire, mowing or inadequate herbicide application.

The underground runners make the bramble very difficult to eradicate and use is usually made of specialised herbicides. These herbicides are most effective in autumn when downward sap movement can transport the chemical to the roots. The bramble can be controlled by cultivation if the rhizome is removed. It is important to make follow-up inspections and treatments, for several years if necessary, in order to ensure complete eradication of this weed from a specific area.

RUBIACEAE

Galium spurium
Catchweed, Goosegrass, Kleefkruid

Height: 1 – 3 m

This species is probably indigenous although at one time it was thought to be identical to the North American species (*G. aparine*), that is a serious weed in Europe, Japan, Australia and South America. It now appears that the South African species is distinct but with some complexes and hybrids that seem to have developed from the American species.

In South Africa this plant is an occasional weed, creeping over hedges, fences and crops, sometimes swamping desired vegetation.

The leaves and stems are covered with little hooks that make them feel distinctly sticky. This makes them adhere to wool and clothing. Broken leaves can severely contaminate wool which is subsequently downgraded.

They should be controlled when young. No herbicides for this weed have been registered in South Africa.

RUBIACEAE

Richardia brasiliensis
Tropical richardia, Mexican richardia, Mexikaanse richardia

Height: 15 cm

As the botanical name suggests, this weed originated somewhere in South America. It has been known in South Africa for a long time, however, and is common in the warmer parts of the eastern half of the country.

Galium spurium

Richardia brasiliensis

It is particularly well-known by sugar farmers but common in many crops and situations without often becoming very serious. It is occasionally a problem on golf course fairways as it can survive the effects of a light mowing and can not be easily controlled when conditions for growth are poor and the uptake of systemic herbicides is slow.

It is not a very competitive weed and is generally susceptible to all types of herbicides. It can also be controlled effectively by cultivation.

RUTACEAE

Ruta graveolens
Common rue, Wynruit

Height: 1 m

Common rue is a native of Europe that was probably introduced into South Africa for its medicinal properties. It has escaped from cultivation and is now naturalised in waste areas and on cultivated lands in the Cape and Transvaal.

It is an evergreen perennial and has a very strong and distinctive odour when crushed. It can cause skin irritations in sensitive people, but is a homeopathic remedy for ailments in the joints.

No specific control measures are recommended for this weed.

SALICACEAE

Populus x canescens
Grey poplar, Gryspopulier

Height: 15 m

The grey poplar was introduced from Eurasia, probably as an anti-erosion agent and for matchwood in the 1920s.

It is found throughout the country on river banks and in vleis, where it forms dense and uniform stands.

Being a hybrid, it is sterile and does not produce seed, but it coppices when cut and regenerates vigorously from root suckers. Mature trees produce a good quality, light, pinkish timber but clumps of poplar must be carefully managed if suitable timber trees are to be produced.

The grey poplar is difficult to control mechanically. Large trees should be ringbarked or felled and the entire root system removed. No herbicides have been registered for the control of this plant.

Ruta graveolens

Populus x canescens

SAPINDACEAE

Cardiospermum grandiflorum
Balloon vine, Blaasklimop

Height: 6 m

A native of South America, balloon vine is now a serious alien invader in many parts of South Africa, especially the eastern regions. It was probably originally introduced as an ornamental.

It is a creeping annual or perennial plant (reproducing only by seed), and can be found sprawling over trees, fences, embankments and similar places. It can grow to enormous lengths and is capable of smothering a tree of up to 10 m tall.

Balloon vine is relatively easy to control. As long as the root is destroyed, the rest of the plant can be left to wither and die. There are no specific herbicides registered for this weed, so the best method of eradication is to dig up the root.

SCROPHULARIACEAE

Striga asiatica
Witchweed, Rooiblom, Mieliegif

Height: 25 cm

Witchweed is an indigenous, semi-parasitic plant which germinates only in the presence of the roots of host plants such as maize, sorghum and sugar cane.

There are several other indigenous species of *Striga* which are not nearly as common, for example, *S. gesnerioides* with more purple flowers, and *S. forbesii* which is a lot larger, are two species that occasionally attack commercial crops.

Seeds of *Striga asiatica* are encouraged to germinate almost exclusively by grasses but also peculiarly, tobacco. The seeds are minute (2 million per gram), with one plant producing up to 500 000 seeds which can lie dormant in the ground for about 15 years. They only germinate in the presence of "strigol", which is a chemical released by the roots of potential host plants.

In unfavourable conditions witchweed can develop and grow normally, but underground. It takes several weeks to emerge, by which time it might have caused severe damage to a crop.

Chemical control is not very successful although some progress has been made with chemicals applied to the host plants as well as the soil. Various cultural methods of control, such as early planting, are used, so that the roots are strong and can withstand attack. One of the other cultural methods is the planting of susceptible plants that are destroyed before the *Striga* produces seed. Crops such as beans, that release strigol but which do not act as hosts to witchweed, can also be grown. This causes the *Striga* seeds to germinate and die. After several seasons of using this method of cultural control, the weed-seed reserve should be reduced considerably.

Cardiospermum grandiflorum

Striga asiatica

SCROPHULARIACEAE

Sutera caerulea
Sutera, Ruikbossie

Height: 30 cm

An indigenous and fairly widespread species that is pioneering by nature and can invade disturbed areas such as pastures and lucerne. In parts of the Cape large tracts of pasture have been taken over by this plant. There are nearly 100 indigenous species of *Sutera*.

It is perennial, semi-woody and has a very strong smell when crushed, making it unpalatable to livestock.

No herbicides have been registered for this weed, but it should be susceptible to herbicides and cultivation when in the seedling stage.

SCROPHULARIACEAE

Veronica persica
Field speedwell, Bird's eye speedwell, Akkerereprys

Height: 20 cm

Originally from Europe and Asia and introduced at the end of the nineteenth century, this annual weed is well known in crops, lands and gardens throughout South Africa, particularly in damp corners.

It is often found in winter wheat, irrigated vegetables and is one of the main weeds in many citrus orchards of the Eastern Cape. It seldom becomes a serious problem as it is not particularly vigorous or competitive.

It is controlled effectively by shallow cultivation at the seedling stage, and is susceptible to the normal herbicides.

SOLANACEAE

Datura ferox
Large thorn-apple, Grootstinkblaar

Datura stramonium
Common thorn-apple, Gewone stinkblaar, Olieboom

Height: 1,5 m

Two introduced species, *D. ferox* from Eurasia and *D. stramonium* from North America, which are now declared weeds in South Africa. They are widespread and serious annual weeds of many crops. They are declared weeds not only because of their poisonous

Sutera caerulea

Datura stramonium

Veronica persica

Datura ferox

259

properties, but because of their tall and aggressive growth habit. In maize for example, both of these weeds are difficult to control, and contaminate the grain; one seed per 10 kg of maize will cause rejection, this being equivalent to approximately one plant per hectare.

The main difference between the species is the length of spines on the fruit (the large thorn apple has the large thorns). Often the stems of *D. stramonium* tend to be purple. Forms with purple flowers were once placed in a separate species, but this is now considered a natural variation. A hybrid has been recorded in the Transvaal.

These species and all the cultivated ones, contain in their leaves the alkaloid hyoscyamine, used in some asthma remedies. The seed and seedlings are, however, very poisonous and human fatalities have been recorded in cases where people have eaten this plant either accidentally or deliberately. The plant is cultivated in Central Europe and South America for the production of atropine.

Being deep germinators, these weeds are not adequately controlled by many pre-emergence herbicides. The most reliable control is achieved with post-emergence herbicides. It is advisable to delay their application as long as it is practically possible in order to catch the late germinating individuals.

SOLANACEAE

Nicandra physalodes
Apple-of-Peru, Shoo-fly plant, Basterappelliefie, Wildebitter

Height: 1,5 m

A native of Peru, this is an annual weed that has spread into most areas in South Africa especially the summer rainfall regions, but with the exception of the O.F.S.

It is a strong competitor and a weed of crops, gardens and waste areas. It is on record as a host to the root knot nematode, *Meloidogyne javanica*.

Apple-of-Peru is susceptible to conventional herbicides and shallow cultivation when in the seedling stage.

SOLANACEAE

Nicotiana glauca
Wild tobacco, Tree tobacco, Tabakboom, Volstruisgifboom

Height: 3 m

Indigenous to Argentina, this annual plant has been known as a weed in southern Africa since the nineteenth century. It is thought to have been introduced into Namibia in horse fodder during the German occupation.

It is widespread, except in Natal, and is usually found on roadsides, riverbanks, old lands and even as a cultivated garden plant.

Nicandra physalodes   *Nicotiana glauca*

Closely-related to commercial tobacco, it becomes a large woody shrub. The seed capsules contain hundreds of tiny seeds which are easily transported by water. It cannot withstand flooding but is highly tolerant of arid conditions as it is said that it is able to obtain moisture from fog. It is common in the beds of rivers that only flow occasionally.

Wild tobacco can cause poisoning of livestock, with symptoms similar to that of nicotine poisoning. Evidently, according to the Afrikaans name, it is well-known for poisoning ostriches. Wild tobacco has been used as a rat poison in Italy and the dried flowers are said to kill cockroaches.

Wild tobacco should be controlled when small.

SOLANACEAE

Physalis angulata
Wild gooseberry, Wilde-appelliefie

Physalis viscosa
Sticky gooseberry, Klewerige appelliefie

Height: 0,3 – 1,5 m

Both of these species have been introduced from the Americas and are now widespread weeds in South Africa.

The wild gooseberry, *P. angulata*, which grows to a height of over a metre, is a common, but not often serious annual weed in the summer rainfall areas. It can sometimes be a strong competitor, but is relatively easy to control, being susceptible to conventional herbicides and shallow cultivation when still a seedling.

The sticky gooseberry, *P. viscosa*, is a perennial plant which spreads into large patches on account of its ramifying underground rhizomes. It never grows very tall (about 30 cm), and is common in waste areas, on roadsides and in perennial crops, in most areas of South Africa. It has been suspected of causing a taint in dairy products. The sticky gooseberry is squatter, tougher and more difficult to remove than the wild gooseberry.

As with most plants with perennial underground systems, *P. viscosa* is very difficult to control, especially in perennial crops. It causes serious problems for South Africa's sugar farmers as it resists the conventional herbicide programmes. Individuals that have escaped, or patches of sticky gooseberry should be spot sprayed with systemic, non-selective herbicides.

Physalis angulata

Physalis viscosa

SOLANACEAE

Solanum elaeagnifolium
Silverleaf bitter apple, Satansbos, Silwerblaarbitterappel

Solanum incanum
Thorn apple, Gifappel

Solanum panduriforme
Bitter apple, Bitterappel

Solanum sisymbrifolium
Dense-thorned bitter apple, Doringtamatie

Height: 1 m

S. elaeagnifolium, a native of the Americas, is an important perennial weed of South Africa.

The silverleaf bitter apple was first recorded in this country in 1952, although some authorities believe it was identified at Wolmaransstad as early as 1919. It was probably introduced with hay and has now spread to large parts of the O.F.S., Transvaal and the eastern and south-western Cape.

It occurs mainly on disturbed soil, neglected lands, in grazing camps, along roads and in water furrows. When it occurs in cultivated land it can completely swamp the planted crop. It is very similar to *S. panduriforme*, but with thorns.

In recent years the government has spent large sums of money on its control, without significant success. Its very extensive root system, which penetrates to depths up to 3 m or more, and its ability to propagate from its roots, make the silverleaf bitter apple an extremely difficult weed to control.

At present no herbicides have been registered to combat this weed. Biological control is showing promise and several defoliating beetles are being studied by the Department of Agriculture. The plants, with as much of the root as possible, should be removed before seeds are formed. Continuous removal will debilitate the plant and prevent the roots from forming shoots.

There are many other species of *Solanum* often referred to as 'bitter apple' or 'wild tomato'. Many of them such as these have thorns on the stems and the leaves. Some of them are toxic with the unripe fruit being more toxic than the ripe fruit. The ripe fruit does not fall off easily and often remains on the plants in winter. The fruit are then spread around in hay or by birds and animals that eat them.

S. incanum is indigenous. *S. sisymbrifolium* was introduced from South America during the Anglo-Boer War and is now a declared weed. *S. panduriforme* is indigenous and found in the summer rainfall region. The fruits look poisonous and have proved to be toxic to cattle. However, black rhino and antelope love them and they are also eaten by French Mauritians without ill effect. The bitter apple is found in such places as roadsides and orchards.

The other species are somewhat more susceptible to herbicides but being perennial, will still require systemic chemicals.

Solanum incanum

Solanum sisymbrifolium

Solanum panduriforme

SOLANACEAE

Solanum mauritianum
Bugtree, Bugweed, Luisboom

Height: 3 m

The bugtree was originally thought to be a native of tropical Asia, but it has since been discovered that *S. mauritianum* is indigenous to South America. It is now a perennial weed causing serious problems in the Transvaal, Natal and parts of the Cape. It was first recorded in Natal in 1862.

It causes serious problems in plantations, sugar cane, and on wasteland as it can very quickly reach a height of 3 – 5 m and shade out other vegetation. It is the principal weed of South Africa's timber forests.

Apart from being poisonous, the fruits act as a host for the fruit fly. They are attractive to birds which eat the berries and transport the seeds elsewhere; peculiarly the birds are not affected by the poison. In young forest plantations feeding birds perch on young pine trees and break the growing tips. It is also suggested that birds, having developed a predilection for bugtree fruits which are available in vast quantities, no longer bother to seek out and distribute fruits of indigenous plants. Large numbers of seedlings often emerge under trees that have been killed by chemical means, from seeds that are unaffected by the herbicide. This makes follow-up treatments essential.

Fortunately the bugtree can be killed easily by cutting, stem painting or soil-applied or foliar herbicides if the foliage can be reached. When mechanically cleared, the clouds of fine hairs that are dislodged contain toxins that have been blamed for respiratory problems in workers clearing these plants.

SOLANACEAE

Solanum nigrum
Black nightshade, Nightshade, Nastergal, Galbessie

Solanum retroflexum

Height: 1 m

The name *Solanum nigrum* is used to refer to a number of closely related, mainly indigenous species that only recently have been shown to exist and which would require specialised knowledge in order to tell them apart. The most common one is in actual fact the indigenous *S. retroflexum*. *S. nigrum* is a European species but it is the name by which this group of species was generally known and which is now considered erroneous.

Nightshade is common throughout South Africa. It is not usually very troublesome although it is frequently found in fields under cultivation. Like many solanaceous plants it is a host to nematodes.

Solanum mauritianum　　　　　　　　*Solanum nigrum*

The ripe fruit can be eaten when cooked but the unripe fruits are poisonous. It is when the berries are green that the plant can be a danger to livestock.

Nightshade is easy to control by cultivation and with conventional pre- or post-emergence herbicides.

STERCULIACEAE

Waltheria indica
Meidebossie

Height: 50 cm

Of uncertain origin, but probably exotic, this plant is widespread in the summer rainfall region, especially in the warmer areas.

It is a perennial weed commonly found in disturbed veld, on roadsides, as well as in waste areas, orchards and similar places.

It has a strong root system and once it has become established, it is difficult to remove by manual means. It should be controlled when small.

TILIACEAE

Corchorus trilocularis
Wild jute, Wildejute

Height: 35 cm

Although this particular species of *Corchorus* originates from Eurasia, there are also some indigenous species which are generally not as weedy.

All of them are usually annuals, reproducing only by means of seeds, but they can survive for more than one season.

Wild jute occurs in the warmer parts of South Africa such as the lowveld areas and coastal regions, becoming a nuisance in crops, gardens and orchards in these areas. Wild jute is similar in appearance to sida except the former has long pods which split open when ripe to reveal the black seeds within.

Blacks eat the leaves of young plants as a spinach.

Wild jute will succumb to the conventional broadleaf-weed herbicides and shallow cultivation during the seedling stage. However, a mature plant is difficult to remove by hand on account of its fibrous stem and strong root system.

Waltheria indica

Corchorus trilocularis

TILIACEAE

Triumfetta annua

Triumfetta pilosa
Burs, Klitse

Triumfetta rhomboidea
Chinese bur, Klitsbossie

Height: 1 m

These indigenous species are quite widespread but are more common in the warmer areas of the summer rainfall region.

They are weeds of roadsides, waste places, orchards and old lands.

The annual *T. annua* is shade tolerant and can invade established crops. It can be confused with *Corchorus* spp.

T. pilosa, which is a perennial, has the largest fruit (about 2 cm in diameter), which like those of the other species, are covered in hooked spines. They can adhere to clothing and can contaminate sheep's wool.

T. rhomboidea has the smallest fruit, being no more than 5 mm in diameter. It is also a perennial and difficult to remove once established.

No specific herbicides have been registered for these weeds.

URTICACEAE

Urtica dioica
Stinging nettle, Common stinging nettle, Brandnetel, Gewone brandnetel

Urtica urens
Small stinging nettle, Bush stinging nettle, Kleinbrandnetel, Bosbrandnetel

Height: 1 m

The above are two species of stinging nettle that originate from Europe.

Although both species cause painful stings they are, in fact, edible, especially when young.

Despite the names, *E. urens* is more common than *U. dioica*. It is smaller and an annual. The flowers are unisexual but are always borne on the same plant and in the same inflorescences. Although widespread, it is only common in the Cape Province, occurring in waste places, damp areas and in orchards and vineyards.

It is very susceptible to contact herbicides such as paraquat and also to pre-emergence herbicides.

Triumfetta annua

Triumfetta rhomboidea

Urtica urens

271

U. dioica is common in Europe but not in South Africa, only having been recorded in the Cape Province. It is a perennial, with a creeping rootstock from which stems are produced. As in *U. urens*, the flowers are also unisexual but the male and females are usually borne on separate plants.

Because of the plant's underground rhizomes, systemic herbicides would be required for effective control.

VERBENACEAE

Lantana camara
Common lantana, Tickberry, Gewone lantana, Gomdagga

Height: 1 – 4 m

This is one of the most serious invader species in South Africa as well as in some other countries such as Sri Lanka and India. It is a native of tropical America and is considered one of the world's ten worst weeds.

First recorded in South Africa in 1858, lantana spread rapidly into Natal and other eastern areas. It forms dense, impenetrable thickets, replacing indigenous plants, increasing erosion and seriously interfering with farming and forestry activities. It is also invasive in parts of Namibia.

The weed varies somewhat in the colour of the flowers and the sharpness of the spines but all these forms, and most of the cultivated ones, are considered to be the same species. The flowers vary in colour from strain to strain but they also change colour as they fade. Over 50 different variants are recognised. It has been discovered that these variants also differ in their susceptibility to herbicides and even to some introduced bio-control agents. New hybrids are evolving all the time and may be parented by even the least offensive-looking garden forms, even supposedly sterile ones. These variants may also be suited to different conditions.

Lantana can be toxic, which, under natural conditions is almost exclusively confined to cattle. It attacks the animals' livers and makes them highly sensitive to sunlight.

The fruit of the weed is a small black berry which is easily spread by birds. Sometimes sudden invasions are experienced when seed is washed down from an infested area in a flash flood and deposited on a flood plain downstream. This, in fact, happened in the Ndumu game reserve after cyclone Demoina in 1983.

Eradication is laborious and expensive. Chopping the dense bushes and then painting the stumps or spraying the regrowth with herbicide are the usual and most effective methods. Foliar sprays on large, uncut bushes are expensive and not very successful. Small plants can be pulled out by hand when the soil is moist.

Lantana camara

273

VERBENACEAE

Verbena bonariensis
Wild verbena, Purple top, Blouwaterbossie

Verbena officinalis
European verbena, Europese verbena

Height: 1,5 m

V. bonariensis, a native of South America, and *V. officinalis* which originated in Europe, were naturalised in the Cape more than a century ago. They are very similar in appearance and habit but the latter is a more robust plant with larger leaves and flowers. They both have tough fibrous stems.

These plants are weeds of gardens, roadsides, waste places and fallow lands, occurring in all provinces of South Africa. *V. bonariensis* is comparatively more common in the Cape, however. They can become a particular problem in lands under conservation tillage.

When young they can easily be controlled by cultivation and with the usual broadleaf-weed herbicides.

VERBENACEAE

Verbena tenuisecta
Fine-leaved verbena, Moss verbena, Fynblaarverbena

Height: 20 cm

Fine-leaved verbena is a perennial plant from South America that was introduced to South Africa for cultivation as an ornamental. It has now escaped and become naturalised throughout the country.

The attractive white and purple flowers are commonly seen on roadsides and waste places.

It would be susceptible to herbicides normally used on roadsides.

ZYGOPHYLLACEAE

Tribulus terrestris
Common dubbeltjie, Devil's thorn, Dubbeltjie, Platdubbeltjie

Height: 10 cm

T. terrestris is an indigenous weed which is widespread in South Africa. It does not occur in the cold/wet areas.

It is a creeping annual, which can spread horizontally into a plant of over a metre in diameter. The seeds have vicious spikes which can cause damage to the feet of stock.

Verbena bonariensis

Verbena officinalis

Verbena tenuisecta

Tribulus terrestris

The plant is commonly associated with the disease 'geeldikkop' in sheep which is a complex problem and not yet fully understood. The plants only appear to be toxic when they are in a wilted condition, such as during a hot dry spell following summer rains. In the Karoo, farmers consider it an essential and life-saving fodder plant, but in other regions it is a serious weed. It is a severe weed of maize in parts of the western O.F.S. for example, particularly on the sandier soils, where it is a strong competitor for the already limited moisture. It is able to germinate even under very arid conditions.

It can easily be controlled by cutting the tap root, but the use of herbicides needs special attention. Control with pre-emergence herbicides is erratic because of the size of the seed and the depth of germination. In maize, for example, *T. terrestris* is easily controlled by post-emergence herbicides when very small. When it has passed about the six–leaf stage, however, specific herbicide mixtures are required for successful control.

PTERIDOPHYTA

DENNSTAEDTIACEAE

Pteridium aquilinum
Bracken, Eagle fern, Adelaarsvaring

Height: 1 – 2 m

Bracken is an indigenous and perennial plant widespread in South Africa and especially common in the high-rainfall areas. It is also a weed in the highlands of East
Africa.

Bracken spreads within patches by means of hairy, underground rhizomes. It is spread
further afield by the copious amounts of spores produced in specialised structures on
the leaves. This method of spore production is peculiar to the ferns.

Bracken is a pest of damp places. In areas of high rainfall, it occurs in the open veld.
Although the plant is poisonous to animals, particularly horses, instances of poisoning
are rare. Poisoning may occur when animals eat the young, curled and tender leaves in
spring or after a fire. Bracken poisoning has been recorded at Estcourt and Ixopo in
Natal and Knysna and the Eastern Province. This weed is highly flammable when dry.

Control of bracken is difficult, therefore systemic herbicides such as imazapr are
required.

Pteridium aquilinum

WATER WEEDS

ARACEAE *(Monocotyledonae)*

Pistia stratiotes
Water lettuce, Waterslaai

Height: 10 cm

Water lettuce is a weed of uncertain origin, although it was recorded in Egypt in 77 A.D. It is now found in tropical areas throughout the world.

It is commonly cultivated in water gardens and aquaria, but has escaped into the wild. It was first seen in Northern Natal but has subsequently been found in the Eastern Transvaal and in the Eastern Cape. It is now a declared weed and a major problem in certain water systems.

Resembling a lettuce floating on the water, this plant has a mass of roots and short rhizomes suspended below. In the centre there is a large number of inconspicuous unisexual flowers. These are capable of producing limited numbers of seed. The principal means of propagation, however, is vegetative.

Water lettuce can block watercourses and provides a habitat for mosquitoes and bilharzia-carrying snails. It can survive periodical drying up of its habitat, but experimental biological control agents cannot survive this, and the effect thereof is therefore eliminated.

Mechanical or hand removal of the plants is usually effective, but herbicides such as terbutryn have been registered for aerial application. If large areas are sprayed at one time, the massive volume of decomposing vegetable matter can cause severe oxygen depletion.

AZOLLACEAE *(Pteridophyta)*

Azolla filiculoides
Water fern, Watervaring, Rooiwatervaring

There are three species of *Azolla* in Africa, but this one which is a native of South America, is the most important one in South Africa. (It must not be confused with *Salvinia molesta* which is also called water fern).

It was brought to South Africa in the 1950s, probably as an aquarium plant. It has now established itself over a wide area from the north-eastern Cape (Hendrik Verwoerd Dam) to the central Transvaal. In these areas it can be found in small dams and rivers and sheltered areas of large ones. It clogs waterways, provides shelter for mosquitos and bilharzia-carrying snails and prevents birds, animals and man from making normal use of the water.

Pistia stratiotes

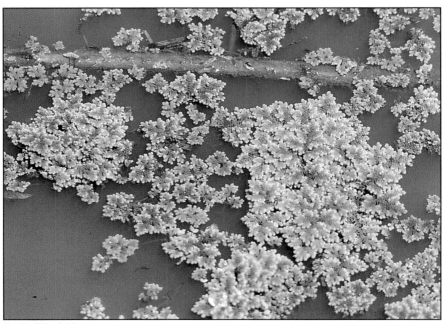

Azolla filiculoides

279

It is a true fern and reproduces by means of simple vegetative methods (division) or can produce spores in the process of sexual reproduction. These spores can be transported by flood waters, birds and animals over long distances.

Azolla has a symbiotic relationship with a blue-green alga *Anabaena azollae*, which is present in the upper lobe of each leaf and is capable of fixing sufficient atmospheric nitrogen to supply all the nitrogen needs of the plant. In parts of Asia the water fern is used as green manure and as a pig and duck food.

No herbicides have been registered for the control of *Azolla* and at present, only physical removal can be recommended to control this weed successfully.

BRASSICACEAE *(Dicotyledonae)*

Rorippa nasturtium-aquaticum
Watercress, Brongras, Bronkhorstslaai, Sterkkos

Height: 30 cm

An exotic species from Europe and Asia that was introduced as a horticultural crop during the early settler days. However, it has escaped into the wild and is now a widespread weed.

It is a perennial plant that usually lives in water but is rooted in the ground. It can clog waterways, increase water loss and act as shelter and breeding site for bilharzia-carrying snails and mosquito larvae.

Watercress is a well-known salad plant.

There are no herbicides registered for this weed and it is best removed by hand.

HALORAGACEAE *(Dicotyledonae)*

Myriophyllum aquaticum
Parrot's feather, Waterduisendblaar

Height: 30 cm

A native of South America, parrot's feather is now found throughout the world. It was introduced into South Africa in about 1919, being first recorded in the Noorder-Paarl. It is now a declared weed and is widespread in South Africa, especially in the south-western Cape, Natal, and in the south and eastern Transvaal.

It is a rooted waterplant that can grow into dense mats, in clear, polluted or brackish water. Although it produces flowers, only female ones are known to occur in southern Africa, reproduction being entirely vegetative.

Apart from blocking watercourses, the weed provides a breeding place for mosquitoes and bilharzia-carrying snails. In frost areas the above-water parts die back producing a

Rorippa nasturtium-aquaticum

Myriophyllum aquaticum

mass of rotting vegetation. Infested water–holes that dry up will rapidly become re-infested when the rains return.

There are no chemicals registered for use on this weed at present and physical removal is the only alternative. Any small piece that remains will take root and grow, so removal must be thorough and cleared areas regularly checked for regrowth.

Research on biological control methods is progressing.

LEMNACEAE *(Dicotyledonae)*

Lemna gibba
Duckweed, Damslyk

Height: 3 mm

Duckweed is an indigenous weed of pools, dams and river backwaters throughout southern Africa.

It is a very small free-floating plant, with each leaflike structure bearing a single root up to 10 cm long. The minute flowers are seldom seen and are contained in small pockets. Duckweed is capable of producing seeds but it reproduces mainly by budding. It favours nutrient rich water and can quickly cover a wide expanse of water. Young plants are eaten by ducks but as the plants mature and decay, they absorb oxygen and give off carbon dioxide and hydrogen sulphide, making the water unpalatable to livestock and unsuitable for fish.

There are no chemicals registered for the control of duckweed but in order to minimise the risk of invasion it is important to prevent the inflow of nutrients (eg. run-off from fertilized fields), and to keep the water agitated.

PONTEDERIACEAE *(Dicotyledonae)*

Eichhornia crassipes
Water hyacinth, Nile lily, Waterhiasint, Nyllelie

Height: 50 cm

Water hyacinth, a native of South America, is now a widespread declared weed in South Africa and is considered the worlds' worst water weed.

It was introduced to South Africa shortly before 1910 and is now well established in all four provinces, especially in the eastern and southern regions. Heavy infestations can be found in the Natal coastal regions, along the Vaal river and in the Crocodile river in the Eastern Transvaal.

Generally this weed is free-floating but it can become anchored in shallow water. Only when it is anchored does it produce flowers and seeds, otherwise it reproduces by runners. The seeds have a recorded longevity of 15 years. The roots are long and feathery,

Lemna gibba

Eichhornia crassipes

helping to keep the plant balanced. The petiole (stalk) is swollen and filled with air to keep the plant afloat.

All members of the family are declared weeds, including the decorative, blue flowered *Pontederia* spp. that are often planted at the fringes of ornamental water features. Indigenous species do not cause problems. In the case of the water hyacinth, lakes, dams and rivers become blocked, preventing navigation and fishing and increasing evaporation. The floating mass can block irrigation canals, pumps and hydroelectric schemes and also harbour mosquito larvae and bilharzia-carrying snails. Cattle have drowned through stepping onto a seemingly solid surface of water hyacinth.

Considerable success is being achieved with biological control. Chemicals are available which can control this weed safely but these are suitable mainly for maintenance treatments or for small patches that pose a threat. Rapid decomposition of large weed masses may cause an oxygen shortage in the water resulting in the deaths of aquatic flora and fauna.

SALVINIACEAE *(Pteridophyta)*

Salvinia molesta
Water fern, Kariba weed, Watervaring

Height: 50 cm

Introduced from tropical America, this free–floating aquatic fern is now a widespread, perennial water-weed in parts of Asia and many countries in Africa, including South Africa.

Kariba weed is frequently found in aquaria and small dams from which infestations can spread to nearby rivers. Under favourable conditions the plant multiplies rapidly, such as in Lake Kariba, where it was first recorded in 1959. Three years later the infestation covered 1 000 km^2 of lake margin.

The leaves of Kariba weed are covered in coarse hairs. These hairs trap air bubbles and thus keep the plant afloat. It propagates only vegetatively, being able to easily regenerate from any small fragment as long as it includes a growing point.

Mats of Kariba weed up to half a metre thick can choke waterways, increase water loss, interfere with recreational use of the water, and provide havens for mosquitoes and bilharzia-carrying snails.

Snoutbeetles were released in 1985 as biological control agents and a number of chemicals were registered for both ground and aerial application. In small areas the weed can be controlled mechanically, but great care must be taken to remove every small piece that could break off and form a new plant.

Salvinia molesta

BIBLIOGRAPHY

ARNOLD, T.H., DE WET, B.C. 1993. *Plants of southern Africa: Names and distribution.* Memoirs of the Botanical survey of South Africa No 62, 1993. National Botanical Institute, Pretoria.

BROWN, C.J., MACDONALD, I.A.W., BROWN, S.E. 1985. *Invasive alien organisms in South West Africa/Namibia.* CSIR-Foundation for Research Development, Pretoria.

CIBA-GEIGY (Pty), Ltd. 1985. *Weeds of Crops and Gardens in Southern Africa.* Seal Publishing, Johannesburg.

HENDERSON, M.D., ANDERSON, J.G. 1966. *Common weeds in South Africa,* 1966. Memoirs of the Botanical Survey of South Africa, No 37.

HENDERSON, M., FOURIE, D.M.C., WELLS, M.J., HENDERSON, L. 1987. *Declared weeds and alien invader plants in South Africa.* Department of Agriculture and Water Supply, Pretoria.

IVENS, G.W. 1982. *East African weeds and their control.* Oxford University Press, Nairobi.

LAMP, C., COLLET, F. 1979. *A field guide to weeds in Australia.* Inkata Press, Melbourne.

MACDONALD, I.A.W., JARMAN, M.L. 1985. *Invasive alien invaders in the terrestrial ecosystem of Natal, South Africa.* CSIR Foundation for Research Development, Pretoria.

MACDONALD, I.A.W., KRUGER F.J., FERRAR A.A. 1986. *The ecology and management of biological invasions in southern Africa.* Oxford University Press, Cape Town.

PHILLIPS, M. 1991. *A guide to the weeds of Botswana.* The Ministry of Agriculture, Botswana.

STIRTON, C.H. (ed). 1978. *Plant invaders, beautiful but dangerous.* Department of Nature and Environmental conservation of the Cape Provincial Administration.

TAINTON, N.M., BRANSBY, D.I., BOOYSEN, P. DE V. 1976. *Common veld and pasture grasses of Natal.* Shuter & Shooter, Pietermaritzburg.

TERRY, P.J., MICHIEKA, R.W. 1987. *Common weeds of East Africa.* Food and Agriculture Organisation of the United Nations, Rome.

VAN OUDTSHOORN, F.P. 1992. *Guide to grasses of South Africa*. Briza, Arcadia.

VAN WYK, A.E., MALAN S.J. 1988. *Field guide to the wild flowers of the Witwatersrand & Pretoria region*. Struik, Cape Town.

VERNON, R. 1983. *Field guide to important arable weeds of Zambia*. Mount Makulu Central Research Station, Zambia.

WELLS, M.J., BALSINHAS, A.A., JOFFE, H., ENGELBRECHT, V.M., HARDING, G., STIRTON, C.H. 1986. *Catalogue of problem plants in southern Africa*. Memoirs of the Botanical Survey of South Africa, 53., 1986. Department of Agriculture and Water Supply.

GLOSSARY

ADVENTIVE – A recent introduction which is now established but still spreading.

AGGREGATE – A non-uniform group of forms or variants within a species.

ALIEN – A plant introduced by man from elsewhere.

ALLELOPATHY – The production and release of chemical agents from one plant that can influence the growth of another.

ANNUAL – A plant completing its life cycle, from germination to ripening of the seed, in less than one year.

APPLICATION – Method of applying a plant protection product such as a herbicide.

AROMATIC – Having a strong smell, especially when crushed.

AWN – A bristle-like projection borne at the end or from the side of an organ; frequently present in the spikelets of grasses.

AXIL – The angle between a leaf and the stem to which it is attached.

BERRY – Juicy fruit with seeds immersed in pulp.

BIENNIAL – A plant that requires two summers for development, with a winter in between. The vegetative phase is completed in the first year and the reproductive phase in the second year.

BIOLOGICAL CONTROL – The use of living organisms to control pests.

BULB – An underground storage organ made up of fleshy leaf bases.

CAPSULE – A dry fruit which opens at maturity to release the seeds.

CHLOROPHYLL – The green colouring matter in plants.

COMMON – Occurring frequently and in abundance within a specified range.

COMPETING =ITOR =ITIVE – A plant that is a strong competitor, is able to flourish in the presence of and often to the detriment of other plants.

CONSERVATION TILLAGE – Reduced tillage practices with the primary aim of preventing soil erosion.

COPPICE – Regrowth from a stump or stem that has been cut down.

COSMOPOLITAN – Occurring in all parts of the world (under suitable conditions).

COTYLEDONOUS LEAVES – In dicotyledons, the first two leaves that appear above the ground.

CREEPER =ING – A trailing shoot which takes root along most of its length or at the nodes, thereby assisting in the gradual spread of a plant.

CULTIVAR – A cultivated variety.

CULTIVATION – The act of growing plants in general, tilling the soil or disturbing the soil mechanically with the specific aim of destroying weeds.

DECIDUOUS – Shedding leaves at the end of the growing season.

DICOTYLEDONS – Plants with two cotyledons or halves in the seed. Otherwise known as broad-leaf plants.

ECOLOGY – The study of the interrelationships between organisms, and between them and their environment.

EELWORM – The same as nematodes.

EVERGREEN – Retaining leaves throughout the year, even during winter.

FALLOW LAND – Cultivated land that is unused or is being rested for one or more years.

FODDER – Animal food.

FRUIT – The dry or fleshy structure containing the seeds.

GLAND – A small globular structure containing liquid, either sunk into the leaf or borne at the tip of a slender stalk (glandular hair).

HABIT – Appearance, outer form.

HERBICIDE – A substance for controlling weeds.

HYGROSCOPIC – Having the ability to absorb moisture from the air.

INDIGENOUS – Native or originating from a place.

INFLORESCENCE – Any arrangement of more than one flower; the flowering portion of a plant.

INTERNODE – Part of the stem between two nodes.

INTRODUCED – Same as alien.

INVADER =ING – A species that is not indigenous to a particular area or the process of an alien plant establishing itself in a new area.

LATEX – Milky juice.

LANDS – In the South African sense, a cultivated field.

MINIMUM TILLAGE – Same as conservation tillage, except that the ultimate aim, for example, may be to reduce costs and not necessarily to prevent erosion.

MONOCOTYLEDONS – Plants with one embryonic leaf in the seed, e.g. the grasses.

NATIVE – Same as indigenous.

NATURALISED – Introduced, but now established and able to reproduce in a new environment.

NEMATODE – Eelworms, minute worm-like organisms that usually live in the soil and can attack and damage plant roots.

NODE – The point on a main stem or branch where leaves or buds arise.

NOXIOUS WEED – A weed proclaimed in the Weeds Act, 1937, (Act No 42 of 1937).

PARASITE – A plant which obtains its sustenance from another living plant (the host) to which it is attached.

PERENNIAL – Plants living for two or more years. They reproduce vegetatively as well as through seeds.

PERENNIAL CROP – A crop that grows for more than one year, e.g. sugar cane, pineapples etc.

PIONEER =ING – Plants capable of invading bare or undisturbed sites and persisting there until replaced by other species.

POD – A type of fruit typical of the *Fabaceae* which splits longitudinally in two valves.

POST-EMERGENCE – Use of a herbicide after the appearance of the weed. (Sometimes used to describe the use of a herbicide after the emergence of the crop.)

PRE-EMERGENCE – Use of a herbicide before the emergence of the weeds (or crop).

RHIZOME, =ATOUS – A stem usually horizontal and underground, and which produces rootlets and aerial shoots.

RINGBARKING – The removal of the bark of a shrub or tree in a complete ring around the trunk.

ROOTSTOCK – Strictly a short, erect underground stem. The term is used loosely, however, to describe perennial underground roots or organs.

RUNNER – An elongated stem growing horizontally above the ground and rooting at the nodes to form new plants.

SEEDLING – An imprecise term, but it generally refers to a plant before it reaches the 6-8 leaf stage.

SHRUB – A perennial woody plant with usually one or more stems arising from or near the ground.

SILIQUA(E) – Fruit of the *Brassicae* resembling a 'pod', more than three times as long as it is broad. The two valves break away from the central portion from base to apex.

SELECTIVE – Referring to a herbicide that can be sprayed over a crop and which selectively controls the weeds without harming the crop.

SPIKELET – The unit of the grass inflorescence.

STOLONS =IFEROUS – The same as runners.

STOOL – A clump of shoots.

SUCCULENT – A plant with fleshy and juicy stems and leaves that contain reserves of moisture.

SUCKER – A shoot arising from the roots of a woody plant, often some distance away from the main stem.

SYMBIOSIS =OTIC – Two or more species of organisms living in a close relationship that is to their mutual benefit.

SWARD – A grass turf or sod.

TAP ROOT – An unbranched, vertically descending root.

TILLER – A side shoot. Once grasses, in particular, have become established, they go through a tillering growth phase before vertical growth commences.

TRANSLOCATION – The movement of nutrients or herbicides in the sap of a plant from one place to another, e.g. from the leaves to the roots or vice versa.

TREE – A large woody plant with a single trunk.

TUBER – A short, thickened portion of an underground stem bearing dormant buds. e.g. a potato.

VEGETATIVE REPRODUCTION – Asexual reproduction through the formation of growth structures that are an extension of the original plant.

VELD – A general term for countryside and natural vegetation, often implying a strong grassy component.

VOLUNTEER – A crop plant that is regenerating as a weed, often in a crop following on the previous crop.

WIDESPREAD – Occurring in most parts of the country.

INDEX TO SCIENTIFIC NAMES

A

B

C

INDEX TO COMMON NAMES

A

C

Y